Super Saints Book I

Journey

to

Sainthood

Founders, Confessors & Visionaries

Bob and Penny Lord

Journeys of Faith®
1-800-633-2484

Books by Bob and Penny Lord

This Is My Body, This Is My Blood
Miracles of the Eucharist - Book I

This Is My Body, This Is My Blood
Miracles of the Eucharist - Book II
The Many Faces of Mary, a Love Story
We Came Back to Jesus
Saints and Other Powerful Women in the Church
Saints and Other Powerful Men in the Church
Heavenly Army of Angels
Scandal of the Cross and Its Triumph
Martyrs - They Died for Christ
The Rosary - the Life of Jesus and Mary
Visionaries, Mystics and Stigmatists
Visions of Heaven, Hell and Purgatory
Trilogy Book I - Treasures of the Church
Trilogy Book II - Tragedy of the Reformation
Trilogy Book III - Cults: Battle of the Angels
Super Saints Book I - Journey to Sainthood
Super Saints Book II - Holy Innocence
Super Saints Book III - Defenders of the Faith
Este es Mi Cuerpo, Esta es Mi Sangre
Milagros de la Eucaristía
Los Muchos Rostros de Maria una historia de amor

ISBN 1-58002-132-8

Journey to Sainthood

Table of Contents

Dedication

Whenever we begin a new book, or in this instance, a new series of books, we always ask the question: Why has the Lord given us such an urgency to write on this subject?

We are convinced there is a great necessity to impress upon the people of God that we are not hopeless; we are not helpless. We have been given an overwhelming amount of strength by Our Lord Jesus to sustain us on the journey, especially during the rough times, which we seem to be in all the time. We have a lot going for us. Jesus continues to keep His promise, *"I will be with you always, until the end of the world."*

In this book, we want to focus on the strength we have been given through our family, our Communion of Saints. We want to share with you their *Journey to Sainthood.* We needed a great deal of help to bring them to you. We would like to acknowledge and thank those strong men and women who know how important this book is, and have dedicated vast amounts of time and effort, to bring you and us these strong intercessors, our brothers and sisters, the Saints.

Pope John Paul II - A special gift from the Father, our Pope affirms all the beliefs in the Saints which we have held onto, which we espouse so firmly in this book. During his Pontificate, he has made a special point to visit their shrines, to venerate them, and to beatify and canonize many Saints. We thank him for focusing in on this all important part of our Church.

Mother Angelica and the Monastery of Our Lady of the Angels, Birmingham, Alabama - It was in this peaceful, yet powerful setting, this contradiction of a nun running a television network from a cloistered convent, where we have been given the encouragement and inspiration to bring these brothers and sisters to you, our family. The Lord used Mother and EWTN to make this happen. We thank her for her ongoing yes to our work.

The Missionary Sisters of the Sacred Heart - the community founded by St. Frances Xavier Cabrini, our Mother Cabrini. We thank the Sisters in New York who pointed us in various directions. We thank especially the cooperation we received in Italy, first at Sant'Angelo Lodigiano by a group of lay people who take care of her birthplace, and the priest at the beautiful church which was dedicated to her, and then at the convent in Codogno, Italy, where Mother Cabrini began her religious order. The sisters there were an outstanding help.

The Sisters of Charity of Emmitsburg, Maryland, at the Shrine of St. Elizabeth Ann Seton for helping us recreate the life of this powerful Saint, in particular Sister Cecilia of the Shrine, who has been our contact person. But we would be remiss if we didn't give a special thanks to the Sisters of Charity of St. Vincent de Paul at the Chapel of the Miraculous Medal in Paris who have encouraged us for years to make a program on Mother Seton.

The Shrine of St. Leopold Mandic in Padua, Italy -The custodians there gave us hours of time and information, books on the Saint which we were able to use in the telling the life story of this beautiful brother in Christ. They brought us to all the places in Padua which represented a part of his life.

Fr. Yoland Ouellet and the custodians at the Shrine of Notre-Dame du Cap in Cap de la Madeleine in Quebec province, Canada, for introducing us to Blessed Frederic Jansoone and the work he did there. We would also like to thank the Franciscans at the shrine of Blessed Frederic in Trois-Rivières for reliving the life of Blessed Frederic for us.

The Company of St. Angela Merici - Brescia Italy - These faithful followers of St. Angela Merici brought us through the Shrine to their Saint in Brescia, and also to the home she lived in, and the house used by her original company of lay sisters. They continue in the tradition set forth for them by St. Angela, during her lifetime.

And for all the others who have helped us, we love you!

Which do you choose,
Heaven or Hell?

the journey to Sainthood

In the Garden of Eden, the enemy of God did not give Adam and Eve the choice of Heaven and Hell! God did! God created a perfect world and gave it to Adam and Eve, to enjoy and bring forth new life to enjoy it, as well. Being a Perfect Father, knowing it would bring destruction and annihilation of their souls and those who would follow, God their Heavenly Father asked only one thing of them, that they not eat of the Tree of Knowledge.

Today, hardly anyone speaks of Heaven and Hell, of restriction and obedience. Heaven and Hell, if mentioned at all, are mentioned as a joke, a state of mind, a throw back to the those who believed the world was flat. Oh, we of the Twentieth Century are too smart to believe in such things. We have advanced so far up the Tree of Knowledge we dare to interfere with God and His Creation. We have become gods, determining the quality of life, who will live and who will die. We check the unborn baby with a sonogram, see if it will be normal, and make a choice! After all, as the serpent said in the Garden, "You have a choice; it is up to you to make a choice; the choice is yours!"

As we have been researching the lives of the Saints, over the past twenty-three years, we wonder how many Saints we would have had, to save the world and the Church, if their mothers had chosen to bring into the world, only what the world judged - the perfect child! Our hearts and minds go to *Leopold the Saint of Reconciliation,* a Saint dedicated to freeing men from the slavery of sin by devoting his life to administering the Sacraments to them, especially the one of Forgiveness - the *Sacrament of Reconciliation* or Penance. He not only lived to bring this Sacrament, instituted by Jesus to free us from the bondage of sin, his deep heartfelt aim in life was to bring about *Reconciliation* between the brothers and sisters of the East, the

Orthodox Churches and those of the West, the Roman Catholic Church.

He would be considered today imperfect, this Saint who measured barely four feet six inches, his body so frail, the quality of his life, such, it would have been better, he had never been born. Yet this Saint brought about in his lifetime, consolation and hope to thousands upon thousands who came to him in that cubicle of peace, the confessional. [Today, are there not those, sadly within the Church at times, who do not advocate souls going to receive that lifegiving, forgiving Grace from Heaven through God's servant - the priest!]

Another great Saint and giant of all time is Charles Boromeo. Today he would be considered slow, as he was slow to respond and hesitant in speech and in execution of tasks presented to him, and yet he was the trusted instrument of two Popes, one of the great Saints of the Counter Reformation. These Popes trusted him, knowing he would get the job done. And get the job done, he did! It was through his work and determination that the Council of Trent, one of the most determining Councils in the history of our Church, was brought about! If someone had not believed in him, had not seen through his slowness, had tried to hide him away, had judged him unfit to take on the monumental tasks of bringing about reform, he might not have had the opportunity to institute measures in the Church we use till today.[1]

We could go on and on, but instead suggest you read on about God's instruments, His chosen ones, in this Trilogy of *Super Saints*. We only speak of this to you, because we are living in the most dire times of this or any civilization. The train of life has gone wild, so much so, it will go off the tracks and crash, if we do not pull the cord and summon the Conductor of Life, and plead to Our Lord for His Mercy on us and the whole

---

[1]Read about St. Charles Boromeo in Bob and Penny's chapter on him in their book: *Saints of the Counter Reformation* (Saints who truly reformed the Church).

world.

Are you one of the chosen ones of today? Whom do you choose, God or the devil? Which team will you play on? Whose army will you enlist in? You have a choice! God has given you the gift of Free Will to choose Him! Whom do you choose? Where will your choice lead you? As for me and mine, we choose God and Heaven. Will you get aboard God's train to everlasting life? It's not too late. We can make a difference. Believe in God; He believes in you. Look in His Mirror, not that of the world, and be transformed. You are beautiful! You are precious in the Creator's Eyes; He made you and He loves you just as you are and how you can be. Love not the temporarary things of this world which are speedily fading away. We have lived in times before when it seemed the world would come to an end, and God gave us another chance. As we see history unfolding brfore our very eyes, we can see the God of Justice taking a Hand in matters. Be not afraid! Although it appears at times, as if the enemy of God and his cohorts have taken over the world, we are not alone. As Jesus promised, He has not left us orphans. He is with us! Turn to Him; the Good Shepherd will lead us Home!

You can become a Saint and live forever in that place reserved for you in the Kingdom; for there is a Heaven, and God wants you to be with Him for all time. This had been His Plan before you were born, to have you with Him, for all eternity. What an exciting tomorrow we have to look forward to. The more we read about the Saints, the more hope we have for you and the world. The Saints never asked *why* but *how* they could do God's Will, and they said Yes! *We love you!*

St. Frances Xavier Cabrini

"We were sent here by the Holy Father...we cannot go back!"
There is a time and a season...

Times were hard, and the land cruel and unyielding, so when the people of Italy heard of the promised land, the New World, they packed what little they had, left their beloved mountains and roots, and left to begin their dream for a better life. Not even the hot, sweltering holds of the poor steamers they traveled on, could dampen their hopes and expectations. As they spotted the Statue of Liberty, all their sacrifices - the lack of sanitation aboard ship, the weeks of family and friends sick from the pitching and heaving caused by the turbulent waves rocking the ship, little food and less water, no air, no light, endless days and nights, all faded. Before them, behind the beautiful lady was the magnificent skyline of their new home, New York City. Not even being herded like so much cattle onto Riker's Island discouraged them. They had hope!

But they were to discover this land of the free was not free for everyone; everyone was equal but some were more equal; unlike their Irish brothers who had come a little before them, they did not know the language; therefore they did not understand Americans and Americans did not understand them. This was mistaken for ignorance and they were treated as second-class citizens. But they were people coming to a land of opportunity, willing to work. I remember my mother saying, "As long as you have your hands and feet, you will never starve. Remember, as long as it is honest, no job is beneath you."

The dream became a nightmare, with the unscrupulous taking advantage of the innocent; unable to defend themselves, Italian immigrants worked in sweat shops - making slave wages, and lived under sub-human conditions. Something had to be done about it!

Left:
**St. Frances Xavier
(Mother) Cabrini
Patron Saint of
Immigrants**

Right:
**Birthplace of
Mother Cabrini
in Sant' Angelo
Lodigiano**

Left: **Mother Cabrini
was a mother and
teacher**

Hands across the Sea!

Our story begins with St. Frances Xavier Cabrini. Born in northern Italy in 1850, thirty nine years later, in 1889, she would sail for the United States, the first of many voyages she would make in her sixty seven years of service to the Lord. She is the first American citizen to be raised to the Communion of Saints, a member of the Church Triumphant. The story of Mother Cabrini, as she has been called throughout the Twentieth Century, is very simple. The Lord asked her to do something; she said yes. Although it sounds simple, it was by no means an easy task. Someone had to take care of the Italian brothers and sisters in the United States; she saw the need and filled that need. The living out of that commitment is what made her a Saint.

We travel to the northern part of Italy, east of Turin and south of Milan, to the little farming village of Sant' Angelo Lodigiano to find the birthplace of our future Saint, Frances Xavier Cabrini. She was born in that small rural community on July 15, 1850, the thirteenth in a family of thirteen children. She was the youngest and the last of the family of Stella and Agostino Cabrini, saintly parents. She was baptized the same day or the following day, given the name Maria Francesca, and in later years when she became a religious, she added Saverio (Xavier) to her name, after her most special Saint, Francis Xavier, who evangelized in India.

There were many unusual, unexplainable, or what we would term miraculous occurrences in the life of Mother Cabrini. *The very first one happened on the day she was born.* On the modest little farm of the Cabrinis, a flock of doves settled in the back yard of their home. This was extremely unusual because doves never settled in this area; pigeons yes, doves no. Her father, Agostino, a simple man, had no idea what it signified, so he tried to shoo them away. They wouldn't budge. This was the beginning of many special gifts and signs given to this selfless servant of God. Humble, she never gave any importance to these gifts. But she never denied them either.

Her mother and father were holy people. They taught their children everything they knew about the Church and their Faith. The children especially looked forward to their father reading them stories on the Lives of the Saints. They all gathered around him, as he spun tales of these brothers and sisters in Christ who had passed the test of time, had been washed in the blood of the Lamb, and were part of the Church Triumphant. This was the family into which this future Saint was born.

Frances was frail all her life, which accounted for her father rushing her off to Church to be baptized right after her birth. He feared she might not live. Isn't it just like the Lord to choose someone who's weak to do the work of ten strong people? She was in good company. Most of our powerful women in the Church have been sick all their lives, like St. Teresa of Avila, Catherine of Siena, Mother Angelica, just to name a few. People were amazed at her remarkable energy.

Frances was the youngest; what with her mother having so much to do and because of the toll that years of caring for the family had taken on her, little Frances was assigned to Rosa, the oldest girl, who was fifteen years old. It was a good choice in that Rosa had dreamed of becoming a nun, as well as a school teacher. She taught little Francesca, or *Cecchina*, (as she was called because she was so delicate), everything she knew. Rosa was an excellent teacher, and so Francesca had the gift of private tutoring. She received an excellent education - gaining both secular and religious values from her sister.

Rosa became her confidante, as well as her teacher and second mother. She could tell Rosa anything. Francesca told her about her hunger to go to China as a missionary, giving credit for this burning desire to the stories her father had told the family on cold winter evenings, about the brave missionaries and their fervor and desire to work in the Missions.

We believe that Francesca was infused with a great love of Jesus and the Holy Family, but her family's love of the Church and their influence on her enriched it. She had a longing to embrace Our Lord Jesus in the Eucharist. In those days, the acceptable age to receive First Holy Communion was twelve. But this was a terrible hardship, as Frances had an urgency to be joined to Jesus in this Sacrament. Couple this with the fact that she knew her Catechism extremely well, thanks to Rosa's teaching, the bishop could do nothing short of giving her permission at age *nine* to receive her First Holy Communion. We believe the Bishop secretly believed as the future Pope St. Pius X did, who in his pontificate brought about the practice of children receiving the Eucharist at an early age.

There's nothing written about Francesca's reaction to the gift of receiving Our Lord Jesus for the first time. Our Little Flower, St. Thérèse of Lisieux, wrote beautifully about the emotional and spiritual feelings she experienced when she was given that first *"Sweet Kiss of Jesus."* Let it suffice to say she loved Jesus so much that two years later Francesca requested from her Parish priest, permission to make a vow of virginity. He questioned her extensively before giving permission, and then allowed it for one year, to be renewed at the end of the year. Francesca kept that vow her entire life.

Although she wanted to be a missionary, her parents felt that a vocation of a school teacher, following in the footsteps of Rosa, would be better for her. So they sent her to a convent school in Arluno, where she excelled. She remained there until she was eighteen, at which time she earned her teaching credentials and began teaching in the village school at Sant' Angelo. She did very well there, and the children loved her. She was not aware of it, but she was preparing herself for the life she would lead as a religious. She was learning how to mother and nurture children, one of her major attributes by which the Lord would draw young girls to her Ministry. Whatever she did, it was with her goal of becoming a Missionary for Christ in India or China, or wherever the Lord called her. She knew that meant entering a religious order.

Her temperament throughout her entire life was one of

"Let's get on with it." To that end, as a young girl, she applied to various religious orders for acceptance. Despite her energy, she was turned down, because of poor health. She couldn't understand how they couldn't see what an asset she would be to their communities, how she wanted to serve God so passionately. But she was always a woman of obedience. Like all the Saints and other Powerful Men and Women we have researched, Francesca Cabrini ranked *obedience* as the most important virtue she could practice and required the same virtue from all who worked in the Lord's Vineyard through her.

A plague of Smallpox hit the village. Francesca and Rosa worked tirelessly helping the victims of the epidemic. Francesca contracted Smallpox, but was never afflicted with permanent signs of the disease. When she recovered, she was sent to another small village, Vidardo, to take the place of a teacher who had fallen ill. It was there she met Fr. Antonio Serrati, who became a lifelong friend and advisor. He could see in Francesca what others may have missed, her love of Jesus manifested in her serving His suffering children. He may have seen the Lord's plan for her even when she could not. He was her confidante; but he was also very straight with her. When she shared her desire to be a missionary in China, he dismissed it immediately with "You're too weak for such a life." Basta cosi! (end of story!) He may have judged she thought it romantic to be a missionary in the fields of China. Or he may have been given infused knowledge as to the mission fields to which she *would* be called, and in which she would accomplish great things for the Lord.

We have seen, when the Lord has souls who are willing to go anywhere or do anything for His Glory, He moves them like chess pieces in the great chessboard of Salvation. Don Serrati was transferred to the small village of Codogno, which had an orphanage which was not being handled well at all. He thought this would be a perfect place for his newfound compatriot in the Lord, Francesca Cabrini. He asked her to come and work in the orphanage. It was called the House of Providence. This move was to prove providential for Francesca, in that it was here she began her community of Missionaries of the Sacred Heart, and where her headquarters remained throughout her life. Through this move, she was also given the experience of working in a field where the Lord would call her and her community, working with orphans and children throughout the world.

She walked into a situation where there were many problems as well as intrigues and infighting. The woman who had financed the orphanage, made herself head of it, and was causing many problems, which was the main reason Francesca was asked to come. But she couldn't let the woman know she was taking over. We don't know, whether Mother Cabrini always had a strong will or if she developed this tenacity, for which she was known all her life, through the trials she endured, working in the orphanage in Codogno. Whatever the case, this job gave her the strength she would need to walk through other trials in her life. It became her novitiate. She put up with all the eccentricities of the woman who had been running the orphanage for six years, as a sign of obedience to the priest and the Bishop of Lodi, whose diocese she was in. On the feast of the Triumph of the Cross, September 14, 1877, she took her vows as a religious, and was officially put in charge of the orphanage.

This actually caused more problems than it meant to solve. The former owner (who had been in charge of the orphanage), became unglued. Francesca's problems were multiplied. Finally, the bishop closed the orphanage. It was inevitable. But we think the Lord had plans for Francesca, which entailed her moving along. The bishop was really inspired by the Holy Spirit, when he sat Francesca down in his office and told her, since he did not know of any missionary order, and she desired to become a missionary, she should found a missionary Congregation herself.

The Beginnings of the Missionary Sisters of the Sacred Heart

Francesca was a good poker player. She never once showed her feelings. She told the bishop, *"I will look for a house."* But we have to believe that her heart jumped a mile high when she was given this singular honor by the bishop. Possibly she jumped in the air as she left the bishop's office, or waited until she got back to her quarters where the other seven sisters were waiting, before she exploded with joy. But we know what we know - she was excited. And now, as the mother superior of a religious community, which she named Missionary Sisters of the Sacred Heart, she was given the title **Mother Cabrini**.

She found an abandoned convent in back of a Franciscan friary in Codogno which needed a lot of work. But this is where the Lord told her she and the sisters should be. The bishop gave his consent, and the sisters moved in the same day, before any of the badly needed repairs were done. It was as if she were afraid she would wake up to find this was all a dream, or that the bishop would change his mind, if she didn't move in immediately. That day became the official date of the beginning of the Order.

She moved quickly, because she wanted papal approval of the order. She opened an orphanage, then a school in another town. She wanted to build credentials and numbers of sisters which she could present in Rome to open a convent in Rome. By 1887, she had five convents in the Lombardy region of Italy and anticipated missions all over the world. She asked permission from the Vicar General of Milan to go to Rome and was given it. In September 1887, she and another sister went to Rome to do whatever it would take to bring their little community to the attention of His Holiness and the Vatican.

I guess when the Lord wants something done, it becomes obvious by how quickly it gets accomplished. True, Mother Cabrini was a mover and shaker, but she was unknown in Rome. What was accomplished in a very short period of time without money, by the way, could only have been the work of the Lord. A Cardinal Parocchi told them not to even consider what they had in mind when he first met with them.   However, on his second meeting with them just two weeks later, he not only gave them permission to open one convent, but *two convents* in Rome.

But a strong lesson is to be learned in the way the audience with the Cardinal went on this second visit. He pre-emptied his statement with a question: *"Are you willing to obey?"*

That might have been a difficult one for Mother Cabrini to swallow because she wanted this badly. But obedience had been a major virtue in her life, so her answer really came easily:

"Without a moment's hesitation, your Eminence."

That was all the Cardinal needed. He had a strong worker here who would do great things for God, but her most exceptional virtue, as far as he was concerned, was that of obedience. He replied, *"Then, instead of opening one convent in Rome you will open two..."*

Well, if you think she went into orbit when the bishop gave her permission to begin an order in 1880, this time she did everything but levitate. She had been given the opportunity, she and her community needed to allow her work to be known, where it had to be known, in the Vatican circles. Getting the work done, which would be the hardest goal to accomplish, was never a problem for Mother Cabrini. She just barreled ahead, not accepting any barriers which might be placed in her way, or the task at hand. She knew the Lord was asking something of her, and her answer was always a resounding yes!

The New Mission Fields in the West

The Lord was grooming her for her great mission, about which she had not a clue. Like it or not, she still had that agenda which had been with her since she was a child - she pictured herself in the missionary fields in China. But a new missionary field had been developing in the last fifty years or so about which she was not informed, because it had nothing to do with her or her sisters. Or so she thought! On the other side of the world, in the United States, Italian immigrants were suffering. They were in a foreign environment, held back by the lack of knowledge of the customs and language of the people of the United States, were attacked and being taken advantage of by unscrupulous employers and landlords who saw in these people, laborers who could be mistreated and misused because they were trying to make a place for themselves in competition with a vast sea of other immigrants, all trying to do the same.

A hero of the Italian Immigrants was Bishop Scalabrini, bishop of the diocese of Piacenza, who had committed himself to helping the plight of the unfortunates who had gone overseas in the hopes of a better life, only to find that their life had become a living hell. He had begun an Order of Missionaries to care for the immigrants. But the need far exceeded the help. The more he heard about Mother Cabrini and her sisters, the more he felt they were just what was needed to help ease the very explosive situation mushrooming on the other side of the great ocean.

Bishop Scalabrini asked Mother Cabrini to meet with him in Rome. She was not prepared for his request, however. He explained the plight of the Italian immigrants in the United States. He asked her to join him in this great work, by sending some of her sisters to New York to open a convent, school or orphanage, anything. But as much as she sympathized with their dilemma, her eyes were on the other side of the world in the Far East.

She did not turn him down immediately. She courteously weighed his request. She clearly wanted nothing to do with it, and so after a respectable time, she turned him down and never gave his proposition another thought. However, just because Francesca Cabrini had not jumped to the fore, and had put the problem out of her mind, didn't make it go away. While she forgot about it, Bishop Scalabrini, who lived with it night and day, had not. To the contrary, it was escalating and so was his urgency to begin turning it around. Bishop Scalabrini was not without friends. The Archbishop of New York, an Irishman by the name of Corrigan, was feeling pressure from the Vatican, to resolve the problems of the Italian immigrants.

We cannot even begin to describe what was happening to

young girls in New York. Many of them took to the streets, as their parents could not feed them. They were left to their own devices, or because of their innocence to those of very depraved people. The problem was reaching epidemic proportions. Archbishop Corrigan had been offered a home and some financing by an Italian noble lady, for a group of nuns to come to New York to open an orphanage for Italian girls who were homeless. He wrote to Mother Cabrini, at the request of Bishop Scalabrini and invited her and her sisters to come to New York to open the orphanage.

Although she didn't want to do this, she couldn't turn down the Archbishop of New York, at least not without some backing. She prayed. She discerned. She asked her community. Finally, she decided to ask the Holy Father. Let him make the decision. She would abide by whatever wisdom the Holy Spirit gave him about this matter. What Mother Cabrini didn't know was that she was playing right into the hands of the Lord. The Pope already knew the problem of the Italians in New York. So while it was not necessarily fair to Mother Cabrini, when she went to have her audience with the Pope, he was fully aware of the problem and was desperate to have people go there to alleviate the difficulty. The Lord had already told the Pope what He wanted.

His Holiness listened respectfully to Mother Cabrini as she shared her dilemma - She wanted to go to the missions in China, but she felt a great pull from various sources to begin working with the Italian immigrants in New York. She needed his help to make her decision. Our great Leo XIII looked at this zealot for the Faith, and smiled as he told her, *"You must not go to the East, but to the West. Your mission will be in America to help the Italians and to make your country loved."* True to her vow of obedience, she accepted the Holy Father's statement as the final word on the subject. She never once mentioned the Orient again.

She had never traveled as far as she was anticipating. She had to go back to Codogno to put things in order. She would be gone for months, at least. She had to get the sisters there and throughout Lombardy prepared to continue on vigorously without her physical presence. When she left Rome, she had letters of recommendation from all the important cardinals, as well as one from His Holiness. She was well-armed for what lay ahead.

"Your Mission will be in America."

There were many obstacles Mother Cabrini had to overcome, on her voyage to the New World. The first adversity she had to conquer was the Atlantic Ocean. She'd had a bad experience as a child, where she fell into the river in search of some little dolls which had fallen from a ledge into the water. She was saved from drowning by her Guardian Angel, but he had never taken her fear of water. She was now going to tackle one of the largest bodies of water in the world, and not the most pleasant. In addition, she left on March 19, the Feast of St. Joseph, smack in the middle of the winter months, which are the most fearful ones in which to attempt to cross the Atlantic. She and her sisters were extremely sick during the crossing, but she never let on. She walked around, trying to cheer them up, as well as some of the other 1500 Italians aboard ship, most of whom had never made a transatlantic voyage before.

When they finally arrived in New York, some of Bishop Scalabrini's priests met them and gave them dinner at the rectory. Everything went well until the Sisters asked to go to their convent. That's when they had the first inkling that all was not as had been presented to them. They had no convent! Not only that, they didn't even have a place to stay that night. The priests brought them through the city to a series of rooming houses, one worse than the other. When they finally found one that met their pocketbook and didn't look too bad, they took it. But they were in for a surprise. The mice and bugs waited until they had paid for the room before they came out to meet them. Mother and her little brood spent that night in a terrible position, sitting on wooden chairs trying to defend themselves from the attackers.

The priests of Bishop Scalabrini's community could not explain why the sisters had no convent to greet them upon their arrival. They hemmed and hawed over where the glitch was. They were sure the Archbishop would be able to unravel the mystery. To that end Mother Cabrini prayed all night to the Sacred Heart, as she sat on the hard chairs, protecting her girls from the New York vermin. They also offered their Mass and Communion that their meeting with the Archbishop of New York would turn out better than this, their first day in the United States.

But when the first words the Archbishop said to them were *"How is it that you are here? I wrote you not to come at this time."* Mother Cabrini almost lost it. The Archbishop covered his tracks by explaining the offer for the convent and orphanage and the funds suddenly disappeared. The truth as related later on was that he had a falling out with Countess Cesnola, the benefactress, and the funds were not forthcoming. There was no orphanage! There were many students for the school; however, no school building. The Archbishop could not see anything but that the sisters return to Italy on the same boat which had brought them to New York. The nuns became almost ill at the prospect of another trip across the ocean like the one they had just endured.

No one knew with whom they were dealing, however; not the sisters, not the Archbishop of New York. We don't know if Mother Cabrini had ever spoken to a bishop in the way in which she was about to address the Archbishop. To his suggestion that they go back to Italy on the same boat, she responded:

"We were sent here by the Holy Father, Your Excellency and we cannot go back. We have been entrusted with a special duty and we must fulfill it." He asked for her letters of credit. Mother Cabrini had been very thorough before she left Rome. She had gotten letters from various cardinals, bishops, and her trump card, a letter from the Pope, explaining the urgency of their mission. Archbishop Corrigan backed down. *"Of course you will remain; it is the Holy Father's wishes."*

Left: *The bedroom of Mother Cabrini in Codogno, Italy. It was in Codogno that she founded the Missionary Sisters of the Sacred Heart of Jesus*

Right:
Audience with Pope Leo XIII He told Mother Cabrini, "Your mission will be in America to help the Italians and to make your country loved."

Below: *Mother Cabrini assisting the Italian immigrants in America*

Below: *Mother Cabrini in Glory*

"We have been entrusted with a special duty..."

Mother Cabrini wasted no time ingratiating herself to the Countess who had originally made the offer. Within a few weeks, she had the money and the building to be used for the orphanage and school. In the meantime, they began a school using rooms of a local church: the choir, sacristy and the body of the church. It was not easy; but by the time they had the building, they had a large enrollment of students.

Let's look at the situation in New York at the end of the Nineteenth Century, or 1889, when Mother Cabrini and her sisters arrived. There were far too many Italians in the city with nowhere near enough church facilities. They didn't have but five Italian churches and nineteen priests. It is said that ten of those priests had left Italy on account of questionable behavior in their native land. There were an estimated 50,000 Italians in New York City alone; with no more than 1200 attending Mass on a regular basis.

Add to that the fact that there were no schools, hospitals or orphanages to handle problems, and you can understand the great need for someone like Mother Cabrini and her Missionaries of the Sacred Heart. However, there was another problem. There were Polish immigrants, as well as Ukrainians, Slovaks, Croats and Czechs. Who was going to take care of them? Archbishop Corrigan felt that it was the duty of the people of substance of each nationality to take care of their own. There was no way that the Church could handle such a large taking.

But while his thinking was rational, it was not logical. There were not enough people of substance to give money for each nationality, and the immigrants who needed the help had no money. There was a whole world out there who needed help; if they decided to wait until there was enough funding to handle each minority group, nothing would ever happen. Mother Cabrini's mandate from His Holiness had been to look after the people of her own country. That's what she did.

She prayed that others would come and reach out to the

immigrants from their own countries, which they did by the way. Strangely enough, most of the benevolent works done in New York, Chicago, Philadelphia and other big cities was done by religious orders of the Church, with little or no help from the city or state agencies. So in effect, what we're saying here is that the Lord saw a need, and used His great army of the Church Militant to fill the need. Their greatest source of support was the Lord Himself. Praise Jesus!

By the time Mother Cabrini returned to Italy four months later, she had successfully put the school and orphanage into place in New York, and her sisters were running them very well. She had never had any intention of returning to the Holy Father defeated and a failure. If she would have had to stay there for a year, she would not have returned to Rome without news of a success for His Holiness. As a sign of her triumphant return to Italy, she brought with her the first two American postulants.

Towards the end of that year, 1889, she had an audience with His Holiness, Pope Leo XIII. He congratulated her on the work her community was doing with her at the head, and gave her a future mandate as well as a prophecy. He said he wanted the Missionaries of the Sacred Heart to extend the Kingdom of God to all the world. Mother Cabrini took these words from His Holiness very much to heart. She knew she had to do whatever was humanly or spiritually possible to attain the goals the Holy Father had given her.

Although Mother Cabrini had only spent four months in New York, she made miraculous strides for the Church of the Italians there. She was considered a major player, especially when it came to real estate. Everybody knew she was bursting at the seams at her little school down on White Street. She needed more space. The Jesuits wrote her a letter while she was still in Italy. There was a beautiful piece of property which they owned on the Hudson River, called West Park or Manresa, which they were willing to sell her at a reasonable price. She recalled as she read their letter that the Archbishop of New York, Archbishop

Corrigan had recommended that place as being perfect for a novitiate that Mother Cabrini wanted to build. So she sailed back to New York in order to complete the transaction.

Mother Cabrini immediately went to the site of the property being offered for sale by the Jesuits. She loved it; it was perfect. She commented, how it would not only make a great novitiate, but also the children from the city would be so happy running around, breathing in fresh air, playing on these grounds. There was only one problem, the property had no water. They could only draw water from the Hudson River, which, while it was being done to a degree, was not practical. Mother Cabrini smiled and responded, "It doesn't matter. God will provide."

Author's Note: *I can't help it but as I write this and even when I'm reading it back, I always find myself saying Mother Angelica in place of Mother Cabrini. When you re-read this chapter, see if you don't think Mother Angelica fits exactly into the story. Substitute the name Angelica for Cabrini and see if it doesn't work. It's one thing to read it after the fact, but when you're writing it, and you find yourself wanting to just write in the name Angelica for Cabrini, it's scary! I'm fitting this into the center of the story of Mother Cabrini so that Mother Angelica won't see it. Don't tell her about it. She gets upset when we call her a living Saint.*

Mother Cabrini bought the property. Then she went full steam ahead moving everything up from the city to this beautiful retreat on the Hudson. Although there was still no water, that didn't bother her; and because it didn't bother her, it didn't bother anyone else. But once they had moved most everything to the new property, Mother called for a Novena to Our Lady. Everyone prayed for Mother's intention. Probably many knew what the intention was. Somewhere about the fifth day into the Novena, she armed most of her sisters with picks and shovels and converged on a certain hill, on the property. Then she told them to dig. As they dug, they prayed.

They were all like little children. One of them squealed

out that the ground had turned dark where she was digging.
Mother shouted out, *"Keep digging!"* They obeyed. Within a
very short period of time, they all exclaimed that water was rising
up out of the ground. They dug into a spring of fresh water. To
this day, that water keeps flowing and provides the property with
ample water. But Mother Cabrini would never call it a Miracle.
It was more like having Good Friends in High Places, she said..

That novitiate became the main headquarters and Mother
House of the Missionaries of the Sacred Heart. It was also the
resting place of the bodily remains of Mother Cabrini until 1959.

"...extend the Kingdom of God to all the world."

One of Mother Cabrini's greatest accomplishments in New
York was the building and running of the Columbus Hospital,
begun in 1892 on the fourth centenary of Christopher Columbus,
and named in honor of the man who had so much to do with the
settlement of this continent. The hospital came about by default.
Another Italian community of nuns was running a small hospital,
and for a reason never explained, left it and returned to Italy.
Bishop Scalabrini offered it to Mother Cabrini.

Mother Cabrini didn't jump at everything which was
offered to her, and even the things she eventually took on were
only done after much prayer, advice from her community, and
from bishops, cardinals whom she respected, and the Pope,
whom she venerated. She didn't' jump into the hospital situation.
She didn't like the idea here were financial irregularities. She
asked a respected Cardinal in Rome, Cardinal Simeoni, his
opinion. He suggested she take the hospital. She kept his advice
to herself, and did not act upon it immediately.

She went to New York to look over the situation first
hand. She didn't have a good feeling about it. But the sisters
reported to her that while they were working in a city hospital,
they happened upon an Italian who did not speak English. He
had a letter which he had been holding for three months because
he couldn't read and couldn't find anyone else to read it to him.
When the sisters read it for him, it contained news of the death of

his mother. The news was not good, but even worse was the fact that it took three months for him to find out about it. Mother rationalized that if he had been in her hospital, at least he would have known sooner, and the sisters could have consoled him more.

Then, to bring matters to a hasty conclusion, she had a dream that she was in the hospital, and saw Our Lady tending the sick. When Mother Cabrini asked Our Lady if she could help, Mother Mary rejected her, saying that She was doing the work Mother Cabrini refused to do.

If that's not a mandate, we don't know of anything that is. In order to do what Our Lady had asked, she assigned ten sisters to begin working in the hospital immediately. So Mother Cabrini went forward, knowing that she was required to take over the hospital, but still being very cautious because the owners of the hospital were not very reputable. Her suspicions were well-founded. Within a few months, the administrators tried to make Mother Cabrini pay for the expenses of the hospital, *because the sisters were working there. That didn't make sense!* She refused, which did make sense; but she offered to take over full charge of the hospital. She was shown the door. But a very unusual thing happened. She refused to leave, as she knew she had a mandate from Our Lord Jesus through His Mother Mary. Well, the patients refused to leave also. This put the owners in a bind because they could no longer care for them.

The Lord saved the day at the eleventh hour. Mother was able to purchase two buildings which were smaller than the hospital and not as well-equipped. But she was able to take the patients out of the hospital they had been in, and put them in the new hospital. She was able also to get enough donations to buy new beds and some new equipment. Granted, the facilities were very meager, but it was a beginning, and from this grew the *Columbus Hospital.*

Mother Cabrini expands her horizons
Mother Cabrini should be named Patron Saint of travelers.

She made more trips to more countries all over the world than we
have made. And all of hers had to be done by *boat*. She crossed
more bodies of water, than anyone we have researched. Her
reputation of success in the United States preceded her wherever
she went. Bishops all over the world asked her to have her
sisters come to their dioceses to begin orphanages and/or
schools. The words of her mentor, Pope Leo XIII were always in
the forefront of her mind, no matter where she might be going.
He said he wanted the Missionaries of the Sacred Heart to extend
the Kingdom of God to all the world. To that end she worked to
the end of her life.

We can't name all the convents and schools, orphanages
and hospitals which were founded by the Missionaries of the
Sacred Heart during the lifetime of Mother Cabrini. We know
she opened many in her native Italy, then went to various parts of
Europe, including France, Spain and England. She continued
opening convents in the United States, in Chicago, New Orleans,
Denver, Pennsylvania, New Jersey and on and on. She went to
Central America, to Nicaragua, to Panama, to South America,
including Argentina, Chile and Peru. Now each one of these
missions could be a chapter in itself. Things always happened
which make the story of St. Frances Xavier Cabrini one of our
most powerful evangelists.

Especially fragile were the missions in Central and South
America. The climate was prone to swing greatly in either
direction. There were places she would go where the red carpet
was extended to her and her community. Then three months
later, she would receive word that they had to evacuate the
mission because the government had become unfriendly, or civil
war had broken out, and regimes had changed. She would not
have minded so much if it had just been her, but she was
responsible for the souls she left in these places.

However, when a situation like that arose, where the
sisters had to flee the missions and leave the country in a matter
of hours, it would take an act of the Vatican to get her back in

again. The Church was always willing to start again, make amends, forgive and forget. Mother Cabrini was not. These were her babes, and although she instilled in them the need for toughness and sacrifice, don't you touch them. You'll answer to this feisty little Italian.

A situation like that occurred in Nicaragua. Some very well-meaning and religious ladies from Granada, Nicaragua wanted Mother to come with a group of sisters to open a mission there. Mother agreed. Now this was the first mission in a country which could be considered somewhat dangerous. Mother Cabrini went to New York to get the money for passage to the country for her and her sisters.

Now keep in mind that Mother Cabrini didn't have any money. These sisters lived in poverty. Someone had to finance all these trips all over the world, and when she brought ten sisters here, or sixteen sisters there, someone had to pay for it. She was always dependent on the mercy of someone with money. But in this instance, when she got to New York, the money was not forthcoming. By now she was used to this, so she didn't let it interfere with her plans. But when the moment of truth came and she still didn't have the money, she had to take action. She went to the Archbishop of New York, Archbishop Corrigan, who by this time, had a grand relationship with Mother Cabrini. He was able to borrow the money she needed and she was on her way.

The voyage could not have been worse. Almost as soon as they got into open waters, thunder and lightning, violent storms on the sea began, to the point where there were times when it didn't seem like the little ship would make it through the night. Mother Cabrini was a seasoned traveler, but she had never ventured into these waters before, nor had she ever experienced as furious a tempest as this. She knew that they were in big trouble. The ship was being tossed back and forth like a stick. Mother stayed up all night, praying the Rosary; the only way her girls would be saved was through Divine intervention. The Lord came and calmed the storm.

Ten days later, they landed at Colon where they then had to take a train across the Isthmus of Panama to Panama City. They boarded a steamer which would bring them to Corinto in Nicaragua, but the steamer was docked for two days so they had to wait to begin this last leg of the journey. Finally, they began moving and sailed along the coasts of the Gulf of Panama and Costa Rica. Four days later the boat entered the Gulf of Nicaragua, off the coast of Corinto. Ten days after they had set sail from New York Harbor, they finished the sailing portion of their journey. The rest of the journey was on horse and buggy to Granada. I know you don't want to think about this, but Mother Cabrini was going to have to make a return trip just like the one she had just completed. Just as an aside, today the trip from JFK to Miami to Managua would take about *ten hours* by jet plane, rather than *ten days* by boat and buggy. And there would not be the sea-sickness they suffered by boat.

Now all the time they were riding from Corinto to Granada, there were people out in the road waving to them, smiling at them. The sisters couldn't get over it. Mother Cabrini was not taken in by any of it. She knew that attitudes can change like the weather. She told the sisters not to be impressed; the people had never seen missionaries before.

With all this adulation, the missionaries were receiving, Mother was correct in believing it would not last. A situation occurred almost immediately after they arrived, which almost made her *public enemy number one* in Granada. She had a problem with what she conceived was immodesty in the women's dress. She accepted that the weather was extremely hot there, but that was no excuse for the way the women were dressed.

The first confrontation occurred when they were having dinner at the home of the woman who had invited them to Granada in the first place. When the women servants came into the room to serve food, dressed in these scanty clothes, Mother Cabrini said that neither she nor any of her sisters would eat until the situation was remedied. The hostess was tongue-tied. She couldn't believe that Mother was making this demand. However, the women were made to wear towels to cover certain areas. They were not happy about this at all. While that frosted some people in the community, they were able to adjust, and so in a little while, the women accepted Mother Cabrini's dress code.

Confrontation number two was a *real problem*. Many of the fathers and mothers of the children were unmarried. Mother would not allow any girls to attend the new academy whose parents were not married. This may not sound like much, but it was cause for major concern. Not being married was a way of life, a tradition if you will. This foreign woman was trying to change their entire way of life, and they were not about to put up with it.

There were staging near riots at the convent doors. They tried to break into the missionaries' quarters and even fired guns to shake them up. But Mother wouldn't budge. She was strong Italian farmer stock, and she was not about to compromise her principles or those of her community for anyone. Finally, after seven dangerous days, where the missionaries were living on the edge, the people gave in and Mother had her way. There were many marriages in Granada immediately thereafter. And then they became her staunchest supporters.

Nicaragua is one of those unstable government situations in which, less than two years later, government troops came up to the convent and ordered it, the school and the orphanage closed within two hours, and all the sisters out of there and out of the country. Needless to say, this was a very traumatic experience for the missionaries as well as the students. But after two hours, carrying what little they could take with them, they walked out of the convent, their faces showing no emotions, but you could see their lips moving in prayer. A girl asked one of the sisters why she was not crying at the prospect of leaving. The nun pointed to the Crucifix she carried with her. *"Why should we cry? With this we came, and with this we are leaving!"*

When Mother Cabrini received a cablegram explaining

what had happened, she advised the superior in Nicaragua to go to Panama where they would be welcome. She was thankful to Our Lord that He had protected all His children. This put quite a damper on the Central and South American evangelization program. While Mother did continue to send missionaries to those two areas of the world, she was extremely cautious, checking into the political situation of the countries, beforehand.

The Missionaries of the Sacred Heart never returned to Nicaragua during Mother Cabrini's lifetime. A request was made in later years that they return and open another facility. This was while Mother was still alive. She demanded that the government pay damages to compensate for the outrageous experience her sisters were subjected to in 1894, before the sisters would return. This did not happen during Mother's lifetime, but it was either a written or unwritten rule that no one go back to Nicaragua unless and until they paid to make up in some small way for what her sisters had been forced to endure. In 1918, the government of Nicaragua paid her demands (after Mother Cabrini's death), and the missionaries returned to Nicaragua.

Mother Cabrini wins over Louisiana

Mother Cabrini loved the people of Louisiana. We love the people of Louisiana. She could not be intimidated by anyone. Her time in New Orleans was proof positive of that. She was asked to work with the Bishop of New Orleans, to rid the state of the tremendous discrimination against the Italians there. There was a large community of Italians living in worse conditions than in New York, if that were possible. The sisters were shocked when they first saw the living conditions.

In addition, there was a great deal of dislike of the Italians. It's not that way anymore in New Orleans. As in the rest of the country, the Italians have become part of mainstream America. We have many Italian friends who live in New Orleans, who have businesses in the French Quarter; they are public officials, professional men and women, doctors and dentists, attorneys, as well as shop owners and restaurateurs. But they paid a high price for their acceptance. Many of our friends shared that when they were children, they lived in the part of the French Quarter, which had originally been a black section. These Italians told us they lived a very difficult life in those days.

At the time that Mother Cabrini embraced the people of New Orleans, the plight of the Italians was at its lowest. There were stories of lynchings of Italians on charges of murdering the chief of police. The bodies were left on the trees and lamp posts as an example.

Researching the life of Mother Cabrini, we found that the reason that the Italians moved into that section of the French Quarter of New Orleans was because Mother Cabrini came into the area and bought an apartment house there. She immediately set up a chapel. The Blessed Sacrament was brought there by one of Bishop Scalabrini's priests and Masses began to be celebrated. The Italians flocked to be near her and her sisters. They were like an oasis in the desert, a dream come true, a genuine miracle.

Mother Cabrini also went to the aid of the Italian people who were being victimized by callous and self-centered politicians. As in New York, being foreigners with limited or no knowledge of the language, they were easily taken advantage of by dishonest and deceitful men. But Mother Cabrini, also a foreigner with no great grasp of the English language, but with the strength of the Angels of God behind her, was not intimidated by these corrupt politicians. She was able to instill the fear of God into them. She was also able to get the police, who adored her, to give protection to the people from the crooked politicians.

Regarding her attempt to help the poor Italians in Louisiana, her historians wrote: *"And when the latter (corrupt politicians) tried to frighten her by giving her a sinister warning, she, a tiny woman, simply warned them of the justice of God and left them speechless."*

Louisianians have suffered greatly, corruption always a way of life they have had to endure for generations. It's an accepted fact, like mosquitoes or humidity. It's just about taken for granted. But one thing they are, *they are Catholic!* They have a healthy respect for God. Tell the people of Louisiana that you are protected by the Angels and they will give you a wide berth. They have a great faith! So Mother Cabrini felt right at home among them. She didn't want to leave them, when the time came for her to move on. No one ever does! She believed she had made a little progress converting some of the public officials while she was there.

A minor miracle took place through the work of the Missionaries of the Sacred Heart. In those days, towards the end of the Nineteenth Century, sanitary conditions in Louisiana were not the greatest. Typhoid fever took many lives. In 1897, an epidemic of yellow fever broke out in New Orleans. The people were devastated. All the schools were closed. But the sisters recalled a similar problem which the Lord had resolved for them in Marseilles, France. It was a cholera epidemic. The sisters had made and distributed hundreds of scapulars of the Sacred Heart. Then they prayed for all they were worth. The epidemic passed, and all who wore the scapular were saved from cholera.

They decided to do the same thing in New Orleans. They hurriedly made as many scapulars as they could and passed them out as quickly as possible, as the epidemic was about to reach plague proportions. They also did the most important thing they could have done; they prayed for the intercession of the Sacred Heart. Sure enough, the Lord came through and everyone who wore the scapular was excluded from the disease.

✞✞✞

No matter where Mother Cabrini turned, the Lord opened her eyes to the many problems the people faced there, whether it be in Spain, Argentina, Denver, Colorado, or good gracious, right in her own backyard in Rome. She had to go to Rome to change locations in one of her schools. When she got there, she became aware that the area in which she was to relocate the school did not even have a church. This is tantamount to sacrilege in Rome, where there are usually two churches on every city street. But this area, Ludovisi, had been the stronghold of an anti-Catholic group who wanted nothing to do with the Church.

She took them on with her characteristic energy. She had an audience with Pope Leo XIII in which she explained the situation, to his dismay and shock. The Pope gave her money to begin construction of a church there. In short time, the Faith was thriving, thanks to the ongoing Yes of Mother Cabrini.

✞ ✞ ✞

Her excursion to Denver, Colorado was something unusual for her. The bishop of Denver had invited Mother to open a house there because of the plight of *Catholics* in that area. He knew that the way to Mother Cabrini's heart was through the Italians, and there were a great deal of Italians unchurched in Denver and the surrounding areas. Mother Cabrini and the sisters found an unusual situation there, something that she might find more in keeping with today's society than in that of the beginning of the Twentieth Century - Apathy. True they worked hard and long hours, and by the time Sunday came, the one day in the week where they could rest, they didn't want to be getting up, getting dressed and going to Church. So they stayed home.

Mother Cabrini could see in this an even greater problem than those who were poverty-stricken. As the parents rested on the Sabbath without giving honor to God, by worshipping at His churches, so the children would grow up with the same mindset. No matter how you looked at it, whether it was poverty or affluence, the enemy of God was working overtime to take the people away from church.

In addition to the problem of getting the people to go to church, there were no Catholic Schools for the children to get a Christian education. Mother Cabrini never minced words. She didn't see any value in any form of education other than Catholic education. She believed that the Lord had to be brought into every aspect of life, and the best way to do that was through the Catholic schools.

To that end, she opened a school in Denver, Colorado in 1903. As she had known and predicted, the school brought the parents out of hibernation. The little church which had been built as part of the school complex filled very quickly for Mass on Sunday, making it necessary for the community of believers to celebrate many Masses outdoors, which was not a problem for the little missionary of Christ.

✟✟✟

Mother Cabrini could very easily be called God's gardener. No matter what land she touched, it became fertile. No matter where she began something, it always grew. By the community's Silver Jubilee in 1905, they could proudly say that they had one thousand sisters in fifty houses all over the world, taking care of five thousand orphans. It was a great tribute to the little farm girl from the hills of northern Italy.

In 1909, while she was in Seattle, she applied for and was granted American citizenship. We believe the Lord wanted to give this tireless missionary a special gift, that of being the first *American citizen* to be given the honor of being raised to the Communion of Saints. In order to be the first American Saint, she had to be American. *Ecco!* (That's it!)

Mother Cabrini felt that no task was impossible. She had an expression, *"I can do all things in Him Who strengthens me."* *No* was not part of her vocabulary. She insisted that if she had received a mandate from His Holiness, Pope Leo XIII or his successor, Pope St. Pius X, it was the Lord speaking to her through His Pope. And if the Lord wanted something, He would make it happen. We can see how Pope Leo XIII gave her the authority to forge ahead as he knew she would get the job done, no matter what the sacrifices. She always took to heart these words of encouragement he spoke to her at different times in her life:

"Let us work, Cabrini, let us work, for after there is a beautiful paradise."

"We want Missionaries of the Sacred Heart to extend the

Kingdom of God to all the world."

"You know how I am devoted to the Sacred Heart. I have consecrated the entire world to It, and you must help spread this devotion since He has elected you for this purpose."

There were many who resented what they considered Mother Cabrini's "pushy" business tactics. When she went to open a Columbus Hospital in Chicago, there were those who accused her of tempting Providence when she undertook such difficult and costly projects. But Mother Cabrini did not worry; she put all her trust in the Sacred Heart.

We feel it's important to put that in this account of St. Frances Xavier Cabrini because we have seen the same determination in a nun whom we have been privileged to work with over the years. In 1988, we interviewed Mother Mary Angelica of EWTN about her life.[1] Bob asked her, "Mother, don't you ever get frightened with this enormous undertaking of a television network, which you started with only $200 in the bank?" *(At the time, the monthly bills were about $500,000)*

She looked off in the distance, thought for a moment and responded, *"No, I don't think that anything ever scared me. I think I always thought, from the time I knew there was a God, that He loved me. I figured He always did and He would take care of everything now. Because, see, I've never known the end of the tunnel; I've never seen the end of the tunnel. I just see God wants me to do something, or God permits something in my life, and it doesn't enter my mind to say, `Why did You do this?'*

*"....So often we toss our ideas to a committee we have in our head (should we, shouldn't we; should we, shouldn't we) and begin to talk ourselves out of everything by reasoning. **Unless we are willing to do the ridiculous, God will not do the miraculous!"**[2]*

---

[1] for our book *"Saints and Other Powerful Women in the Church"*
[2] *Saints and Other Powerful Women in the Church* - P346-348

Mother Cabrini had learned during her 67 years of ministry that the Lord will make something happen if it is His Will. But we must walk toward the open door, knowing that if it is not His Will, He will stop it. But if it is His Will, don't anyone get in His way. It's going to get done. So those who may have had a problem with Mother Cabrini's drive to accomplish what she believed was the Lord's Will, were complaining about the wrong Person. *They should bring their complaint to God Almighty!*

But before we do that, we should consider that in her lifetime, she managed to draw over *four thousand* sisters to her community, open up over *fifty* houses in countries all over the world, and minister to thousands upon thousands of the faithful, not all of them Italian either. When you consider all the houses she started in Latin America alone, you know they were not *Italians* she was taking care of. They were all God's children. To do this, she had to make use of the gift the Lord gave her of being a shrewd business person. But did that come naturally to her? Was she from a business-oriented family? We don't find any of that in her biography. She was a *yes* person. Throughout her entire life, and in everything she did, she said Yes! And for the most part, her *Yes* was to jobs that no one else wanted, until she made a success of them. Then everybody was jealous.

She was observed by historians in the following way: *"...She was slow in learning English and never lost her strong accent; but this apparently was no handicap in successful dealings with people of all kinds, and those with whom she had financial business were particularly impressed.*

"In only one direction did her tact fail, and that was in relation to non-Catholic Christians. She met such in America for the first time in her life - and that was the root of the trouble: it took her a long time to recognize their good faith and to appreciate their good lives. Her rather shocking remarks in this connection in earlier days were the fruit of ignorance and

consequent lack of understanding. "[5]

Let's talk about that for a minute. We're getting to know Mother Cabrini pretty well, even though we have never met. She's our kind of Saint. She was a feisty lady. One thing she never was, was ignorant. But now, regarding this situation with the separated brothers and sisters in Christ, we want to put this as delicately as possible. We love our non-Catholic Christian friends. Many of them love us, but many of them don't. The Mormons call us the Whores of Babylon. The Fundamentalists call our Pope the Anti-Christ. And that's today, when we have *good* relations with non-Catholic Christians.

At the end of the Nineteenth Century and the beginning of the Twentieth Century, Catholics were barely tolerated. There were many areas in these United States where a Catholic could not get a job back then. There are places in these United States where a Catholic can't get a job today. But back then they were not as subtle about discrimination towards Catholics. Today only the media, newspapers, television and magazines are openly vicious in their attacks on the Church. Everybody else is guileful about their discrimination towards Catholics.

We are trying to co-exist with our brothers and sisters in Christ. We would even like to open a dialog by which they can come into our Church. That was the original concept of Ecumenism. But what is, is. And what is today was much worse one hundred years ago when every denomination was jockeying for position in this country, and Catholicism was considered a foreign religion, with an Italian Pope running everything. Keep in mind that these United States have never been a Catholic country. And judging by the behavior of some then and now, there are times and places in these United States where Christians don't even behave like Christians. Mother Cabrini had to deal with all of that.

[5]Butler's Lives of the Saints - Pg 595

Mother Cabrini is such a multi-faceted diamond of Jesus. There are so many things about her we want to share with you. There were Miracles during Mother Cabrini's lifetime. She didn't like to give any credence to them. There were probably hundreds more than we're telling you about, but there were miracles.

An amusing and unusual miracle took place in the instance of a sister who had varicose veins. She had been instructed to wear support stockings at all times. Now she may have done that. We're not sure. But we do know that she got hold of a pair of Mother Cabrini's stockings which were just ordinary cotton stockings and wore them. She immediately felt healed, and by the next day there was no question of her healing. The varicose veins were gone. When she told Mother Cabrini, she looked at the sister like she had lost her sensibilities and responded, *"I hope you are not so foolish as to say my stockings cured you. I wear them all the time and they do me no good. It was your faith that did it. Say nothing about it."*[4] You really have to hear it with an Italian accent.

One evening in September, a fire broke out at the mother house in Codogno Mother Cabrini rushed to the scene; she never stopped praying for a moment. The fire was agitated by swirling winds which threatened to destroy the house which was a dormitory for girls. The young girls were sleeping, completely unaware of the impending danger. The fire surrounded the house. The sisters ran to Mother Cabrini for help Her eyes never left the fire; her lips never stopped moving in prayer. She looked up to Heaven. Then, raising a reliquary containing the relics of many Saints and Blesseds which she always carried on her person, she made the Sign of the Cross. Her prayers were answered immediately. As if acting on orders from Heaven, the fire made a ninety degree turn and moved off, leaving them unharmed.

---

[4]St. Frances Cabrini - Missionary Sisters of the Sacred Heart - Chicago 1965

✝✝✝

A book could be written on the quotes from Mother Cabrini. They are words to live by, food for the soul. These are just a few:

"I travel, work, meet with a thousand difficulties, but all these are nothing as long as you are faithful, observant and generous and prove yourselves true members of the institute."

"In your actions, your words and your suffering, seek always the greater glory of God."

"My good daughters, how prayer enlivens faith and does everything!..."

"He who prays with faith has fervor, and fervor is the fire of prayer....Pray always with Jesus, always remembering that a soul united with Jesus can do everything...."

"Speak often of Heaven to those who approach you, make them love It as well as the virtues which are required before we can be admitted to our blessed country."

"For if you know how to draw souls there by your zeal, your good example and your exemplary religious conduct, you may be assured the gates will be opened for you also."

"O Jesus, I love You very much...Give me a heart as big as the universe...Tell me what You wish that I do, and do with me as You will."

✝✝✝

Mother Cabrini died on December 22, 1917 in the convent in Chicago. Sadly, there was no one with her when she died, or at least there were no humans with her. We know that Our Lord Jesus, Mother Mary, all the Angels and Saints were there to welcome her into the Kingdom. She was probably escorted by tens of thousands of Italian immigrants who had gone to Heaven as a result of the work of Mother Cabrini and her sisters all over the world.

But it's sad there were none of her sisters at her bedside to sign her, to pray her out of this world. The sadness was not for her; she had exactly what she wanted as the Angel of Death took her by the hand, up to the gates of Heaven. She had her Heavenly family with her. It was sad for those whom she left behind. It was their loss not to be with their Mother-in-Faith, their foundress, as she left for the mansions the Lord had prepared for her and all her Missionaries of the Sacred Heart.

It may have been some consolation to them that she was preparing for her death. She had slowed down some six years prior to her death. She tried to turn over all the duties of the community to her successor, Sister Antoinetta Della Casa, who became Mother Superior, but when Mother Cabrini tried to resign her office, the uproar from her thousand nuns shouted "*No*" as one, and the Pope gave special permission that Mother Cabrini would remain Superior for life. However, Mother Della Casa took over the duties of Superior of the Community when it was obvious that Mother Cabrini was failing.

For that time, she lived a long life. Today, we say that she was a kid when she died. But that may be because we're approaching her 67 years. But even if that had been a young age in 1917, considering all that she was exposed to for 67 years, in particular the sanitary conditions or lack thereof, in the countries she voluntarily walked into, it is only by the Grace of God that she lasted that long.

We can imagine the confident expectation amidst the sorrow that the body of the foundress would be brought back to Codogno, where the original convent had been. I mean, where else could it be? But as Mother Superior, Mother Cabrini predicted that she would be buried in New York at West Park, the Mother house and headquarters of the Missionary Sisters of the Sacred Heart in the *United States*. Naturally, she was correct in doing that. Because although the Lord sent her all over the world, this is where her ministry of evangelization actually began, in the steaming streets of New York City. Where else should it end? However, although Mother Cabrini predicted where she would be buried, and Mother could not be wrong, that is not where her final resting place is. After her beatification, her remains were moved to Mother Cabrini High School in Manhattan, which didn't even exist when she was alive, for all the world to venerate her.

Will we get any rest in Heaven?

"One day, Bob was complaining to Mother Angelica: `To serve the Lord is not to know any sleep on earth. He keeps you busy twenty-four hours a day, seven days a week.'

Mother Angelica first consoled, `*Well, you can rest in Heaven, Bob.*

Bob asked her, Are you sure, Mother?'

Then she took it back with, `*No, I think God will have work for you there too.* "'[9]

Mother Cabrini probably found this out the first day she got into Heaven. We don't think she even had time to get a convent set up for her Sisters in Heaven right off the bat. There was too much work to do. There are two reasons we say this. The major reason is because that's who she was, a worker. Workers work, even in Heaven. Look at the Little Flower, St. Thèrése of Lisieux; she predicted that she would continue to work in Heaven. Her final prediction was:

"God would not give me this desire to do good on earth after my death if He did not want to realize it...

"If you knew what projects I have in mind, what I will do with things when I am in Heaven. I will begin my mission..

"If God grants my desires, my Heaven will be spent on earth until the end of time. Yes, I will spend my Heaven doing good upon earth...

"I will return! I will come down!"[10]

During her lifetime, Mother Cabrini would never let the sisters talk about the many miracles with which the Lord blessed her personally, and the community in general. She didn't want attention focused on her, but on the work she had to do. But

---

[9]*Saints and Other Powerful Women in the Church* - Page 350
[10]*Saints and Other Powerful Women in the Church* - Page 280

after she was dead, apparently then it was all right, or the Commander-in-Chief (Jesus) over-ruled the Foundress. He was probably the only one who could get away with it.

At any rate, we're told that over 150,000 petitions and reports of favors granted through the intercession of Mother Cabrini, poured in from all over the world. Remember, hers was a world apostolate! The reaction from Rome was predictable. The first thing they had to do was to grant a dispensation from Canon Law 2101 which stated that the cause for Canonization for anyone can not be opened until that person has been dead for at least fifty years. When the Archbishop of Chicago, Cardinal Mundelein opened the information portion of the Cause for her Canonization in 1928, she had only been dead *eleven years.*

Things moved so quickly that she was declared Venerable[11] on November 1, 1937, Feast of All Saints Day. The miracles necessary for Beatification were lining up, waiting to be accepted. There was no problem picking two, to declare as Miracles towards the Cause for Mother Cabrini. The first was one of her own sisters in Seattle, who was hopelessly ill from a disease affecting the gall bladder, duodenum and the colon. She was on death's door in 1925 after many operations done in Mother Cabrini's own hospital, Columbus Hospital in Seattle. This sister was so far gone she was given the Last Rites of the Church and Viaticum.[12] As soon as she had received Communion, she had a vision of Mother Cabrini and was cured.

The second one accepted, was a newborn child, born in 1921 in the New York Columbus Hospital. By error, a nurse spilled silver nitrate on the child's eyes on the day he was born, which should have burned his eyes and resulted in him being blind for life. Everybody in the hospital immediately began praying to Mother Cabrini for her intercession. By this time there

---

[11]Venerable is the first step in the Canonization process, to be followed by Beatification and then Canonization

[12]Last Holy Communion given to those who are dying

had been many reports of miraculous cures and healings through the intercession of the little Italian foundress. The very next day, the child's eyes were examined and they were completely normal. *Praise Jesus!*

One year and twelve days later, she was beatified, on November 13, 1938. Two new miracles were needed for the Canonization. The Church accepted two cases where medical cures had taken place within days after invoking the aid of Mother Cabrini. The way she worked in life, she worked in death - fast! On January 11, 1944, she was raised to the Communion of Saints, the first *American citizen* to be so honored, and the first Canonization during the pontificate of Pope Pius XII.

People comment to us all the time how fortunate we are to have a Ministry which takes us all over the world to videotape the shrines of Our Lady, the Angels and the Saints. But we think that Mother Cabrini has us beat. We thank Our Lord Jesus for allowing us to go to just a few places where Mother Cabrini touched down on, and to take in the feelings all around us of the love and energy of this most Powerful Woman in our Church. *Praise Jesus for Saint Frances Xavier Cabrini, our Mother Cabrini!*

Left: *St. Leopold Mandic*
Saint of Reconciliation
Apostle of the Confessional

Below: *St. Leopold had the gift of*
Wisdom, many came to him.

Above: *The Confessional of St. Leopold*

Above: *The dream of Saint Leopold Mandic was Unity between the*
Greek Orthodox, Russian Orthodox and Roman Catholic Churches.

Saint Leopold Mandic
Saint of Reconciliation

Saint Leopold, although a multi-faceted Saint who could be Patron Saint of many areas of our life, is best known for that part of his vocation as a Priest, to which he most dedicated his life, the Sacrament of Reconciliation. We believe that the Lord is resurfacing these little known Saints in the United States, at the threshold of the new millennium, to serve as *Role Models* to priests in particular, but to all of us in general.

This is simply the story of a Priest! At a time in our Church where we are sometimes discouraged from going to confession and are told that a general confession once a year is sufficient, when children are made to receive First Holy Communion before receiving the Sacrament of Reconciliation, when sin is down-played to such a degree, as with Pilate, we hear *"What is sin?"* when sin has been replaced by such catch words as *dysfunctional, neuroses,* and we are told *"You're all right; I'm all right,"* along with varied terms of psychosis, it is time to learn about a Priest who devoted his entire life to bring about peace and reconciliation between man and God!

As with Jesus, Father Leopold knew man could not be whole unless his sins were forgiven. He knew and dedicated his life to fulfilling this mandate from Jesus to him and all priests, to heal through the Sacrament of Reconciliation. As Jesus before him spent much of the few precious years left Him on earth, forgiving sins, knowing that only through this Sacrament of Healing would His children know true healing, so it would be with Leopold, serving God to the end in the confessional. Father Leopold was not only a reconciler of sins in the confessional, but, like Pope John Paul II, coming from the Catholic Church in the East, his prayer and action would be to try to bring about reconciliation between the Orthodox and the Roman Catholic Church in Rome. Believing that with God nothing was impossible, Leopold worked tirelessly toward that end, always placing his hopes in God's mercy and power to change men's hearts.

But let us begin at the very beginning. The world was in one of the worst messes it had ever known. The year was 1866; the Austro-Hungarian Empire was about to embark on a series of bloody wars, in an attempt to save the Hapsburg Empire, which would ultimately culminate into a World War, not only encompassing most of Europe, but involving the United States as well. It would cause the loss of American lives alongside those of European brothers - a senseless war that would accomplish nothing except leave a smoldering fire, which would erupt years later into another World War.

As war began in this land which was part of the Austro-Hungarian Empire for seventy years, so God would raise up a Saint who would symbolize peace and reconciliation. Although he was helpless to bring about peace through armistice between nations, he was able to save lives in his confessional providing the penitents a knowledge of a peace and freedom which no one could take from them, a freedom which would follow them to eternal peace and freedom in Heaven. And through that peace, a change of heart. He taught that no matter how much evil there is in the world, no matter how helpless peace seems in this world, no amount of calamities, tragedies or disasters could rob one of this Peace which Jesus left us, the Gift of Reconciliation!

A Saint is born!

Our Saint was born in *Castelnovo* (or better known as Dalmatia) on December 5, 1866. Leopold's father's family were of a long line of nobility of Bosnia. They left Bosnia for Castelnovo, and as this was on the Adriatic Sea, and his grandfather was a successful ship-owner, the family led a very comfortable life from the sea. Leopold's grandfather built a castle for his family; and when his son (Leopold's father) took a wife, he brought her to this fine home, along with the business he would later inherit. As Leopold's mother was also of noble blood, Leopold was born into a life of finery and position. Leopold was groomed to live in keeping with his family's station in life, to carry on the long line of noble ancestors. But this interested him little; he was more engrossed in a nobility of a higher sort, to seek out and follow the path of any relatives who like him, had desired to serve God as Priests. His joy was not to be found in the long line of nobles who colored his past, but in the two ancestors who had been priests.

Leopold was the last of twelve children; a tiny baby, he would not grow into more than 4 foot 6 inches. From birth, he was a sickly child; but what he lacked in height and good health he would possess in wisdom and compassion. The hatred that till this day pits brother against brother and neighbor against neighbor was prevalent at the time of Leopold's birth, a fallout from the hundreds of years of Moslem domination and consequently Christian persecution. Not only would there be distrust and hostility between the Christians and the followers of Islam but among themselves as well, with the Orthodox and Roman Catholic children of God irreconcilably divided. Later grieving over the hatred and division, the hardness of hearts of his countrymen, the bloodshed and heartache that had come about through the merciless years of foreign occupation and the painful schism that had split the family of God, this little giant would devise a plan to bring about reconciliation; he would become a missionary who would lead his, the people of the East back to the one true Roman Catholic Church.

Although as a baby Leopold was so frail and sickly, his parents Pietro Antonio Stefano Mandic and Carolina Zaravic[1] had to wait a month before having him baptized. The name they gave him Bogdan, which means *"the God-given one,"* was destined to become a prophecy; this extremely delicate child would grow into a powerful instrument in the Church's quest for reconciliation between God and His children, his aim forever -

---

[1]In most European countries and Mexico the wife maintains her family name, even dying with that name, for example, Leopold's mother was known as Catherine Zaravic, wife of Pietro Antonio Stefano Mandic.

unity, one family undivided.

Bogdan was not only the product of a noble family, from which he inherited fine manners and a gentle spirit, he was also blessed to have truly Christian parents who recognized in this, their last jewel from the Father, one chosen to give his life to the Lord and His Church. They encouraged him, guiding him on his path to holiness. Growing up, he excelled as a student, seriously immersed in his studies. But this did not detract from his love for his fellow man, always ready to help someone less fortunate than he. He showed an early tenderness toward the poor. A former school friend later testified Bogdan shared his meager food allowance with him because he was poor and did not have enough to eat.

But this love for God's creatures did not in any way lessen or detract from his love for God and his desire to serve Him with all his mind and heart. One time, he heard one of his friends use the Name of the Lord in vain, angrily cursing God, because he had lost the last of his money gambling. Bogdan, crying, gave him what little he had if he would just stop blaspheming the Lord and promise to never again wound his Lord with such language. His parents could see their boy walking farther and farther away from the *temporal* world and closer and closer toward the *eternal* world we all seek. Whenever his parents could not find him, they would go to his room where they would see him, kneeling on the bare wooden floor, praying, deeply detached from the world and its distractions.

Bogdan begins his new life and becomes Brother Leopold

As Bogdan chose more and more the life of austerity, his heart drew him closer and closer to the Capuchin order. The decision was made that Bogdan would enter the Capuchin Seminary in Udine, on the border between Italy and Yugoslavia. Now the Capuchins of the Venetian Province were no strangers to Bogdan or the people of Castelnovo (Herzogovina), as they were responsible for the Catholic Church remaining alive during almost 700 years of occupation by the Moslems, when it was a death sentence to speak the Name of Jesus, no less administer any of the Sacraments or teach the Faith. The day came, November 16, 1882 and it was time for Bogdan to leave for the Seminary in Udine. Bogdan had been their favorite child and his parents could not hide their tears at parting with him. They were also a bit hurt; they asked him if he was not even a little sorrowful leaving them and their home; how could he leave them without shedding a tear? He peacefully replied with a joy they had never before seen, *"How can I cry when I am going to the house of the Lord?"*

Life for Father Leopold in the Seminary was to be one of fasting, prayer and acts of penance and mortification. For example, the habit worn by Father Leopold and his fellow seminarians was constructed in such a manner, as to allow the biting cold of winter to penetrate its loose coarse weave and flimsy shell, chilling the wearer beneath to the bone. Then in the suffocating heat of summer, the habit created an oven-like condition bathing the friars in sweat, at times, and almost frying them at other times. What little sleep was allowed them because of the freezing cold in their cells in the frosty winter months and the sweltering heat of the long days of summer, was interrupted by hours of prayer and meditation. Their dainty sparse meals were barely enough to sustain them. They were limited to twice a day, with nothing to eat in the mornings. What little food rations they had available was further reduced during times of fasting, close to six months of the year. They observed the vow of silence, speaking with permission, only once or twice a week. Their frequent praying took up most of the seminarians' days.

What gave the future Saint Leopold the strength and stamina to obey, in the light of the rejection and alienation he would know in the years to come? Life in the Seminary is never easy; but upon seeing Bogdan's delicate frame and obvious poor health, the Capuchins were sure he would not survive the rigors of the life of the Capuchins. They were soon to be proven wrong, as Bogdan, now Brother Leopold, dug into life with his

Above: *Capuchin church in Fiume where St. Leopold Mandic stayed as confessor to the Croats in 1933.*

Above: *St. Leopold Mandic as a young Capuchin*

Right: *St. Leopold Mandic loved children.*

Above: *St. Leopold Mandic was a man of prayer. Interior of the old Church of the Capuchins in Padua, Italy*

new family, as zealously as he would pursue all the tasks God
and life would hand him.   Seeing how he attacked his daily
duties, his studies and most importantly his spiritual life, his
superiors soon discovered the Lord and His Mother had gifted
them with an uniquely chosen soul.   To confound the devil, he
would take the vows of *obedience, poverty and chastity* on May
3, 1885.

His first year of the Novitiate completed, Brother Leopold
was sent to Padua to study Philosophy and then from there to
Venice to deepen his knowledge of Theology. Although a great
student delving faithfully into all his subjects, his mind and heart,
his thoughts and words never wandered far from God. This little
person was so charismatic and his love for God so electric he
was like a garden of sweet and fragrant flowers drawing bees to
drink of his nectar. He was loved by all and deeply respected.

November 20, 1890, Brother Leopold was ordained a
priest, and became Father Leopold. He did not have the gift of
saying his first Mass in his native Croatia; but instead the closest
his loved ones came to sharing his first moments as another
Christ, *"alter Christus,"* was through a picture he sent to his
family, taken on that day, the most monumental day of his life.
They said that his Masses were truly a reenactment of Jesus'
ascent to Calvary, His Death and Resurrection. Seeing the tiny
Capuchin raising the Host to the Father, his tiny arms aloft with
his King in his hands, a tremor would travel through the church, a
feeling pass from parishioner to parishioner that at any moment,
the curtain would again split in the Temple in Jerusalem, as it had
that first Sacrifice of the Cross. This was how real his Masses
were! There, seeing him adoring his Lord alive on the altar, you
had the feeling this was his first Mass, his last Mass, his only
Mass. Those who celebrated Mass after him, spoke of seeing the
altar still wet from the tears he had shed during his Mass.

The day of his ordination, Father Leopold began his
nineteen year journey from friary to friary, to shrine after shrine,
always intent on doing the Will of God. No matter where he

served, his delight was the ministering of the Sacraments, spending most of his day administering the Sacrament of Reconciliation. The day came when he was transferred to Padua. At first he taught and directed students in the House of Studies. But finally he was relieved of this duty and was free to concentrate on the confessional and the many souls who came to him seeking God's forgiveness. He was so happy!

Then World War I broke out and as always, the innocent suffered the wounds owed to the few perpetrating senseless death and horror on God's people.   As Croatia and Italy were on different sides of the war, and Italy had just suffered a serious blow in a defeat at Caporetto, the Italian government insisted Father Leopold renounce his Croatian citizenship. A loyal son is a loyal son. As faithful as he was to the Catholic Church, he was to the country of his birth; Father Leopold refused to disavow Croatia and become a son of Italy. He was sent to an internment camp in the South of Italy, where he remained under guard from 1917 to 1919. This was the most painful time in his life; he cried as he heard of the bloody strife between his native land and the land where the Lord had sent him to serve. Through all this, he lived under a cloud of suspicion and mistrust.

But all things joyful and horrible, come to an end; only God and His eternal Kingdom is forever. The war at last over, not only the Bishop but all the faithful clamored for his return. Father Leopold was welcomed with loud proclamations; their faithful priest and brother Paduan had come home to Padua and his confessional.

No sooner was he settled there in the Capuchin monastery, he was called to another change, a new assignment! At first, he was a little apprehensive, but turning his life again to the care of his Lord Jesus and his Heavenly Mother Mary, he awaited the Will of the Lord. When it came, he had mixed emotions. He loved the souls of Padua, but he had missed the brothers and sisters of his native land. A piece of his heart always with his beloved Croatia, it would appear he would have his dream; he was transferred to Fiume (Yugoslavia). But that too, was short-lived, as the Bishop of Padua requested he be returned to his diocese. And so the little priest who desired to be with his Croatian family was to know but a few fleeting moments with that dream. His passion to become a missionary was to be fulfilled not by spending the rest of his life far off in some jungle or rain forest, but in the hustling, bustling university city of proud Padua. Here he would remain till his death.

Sometimes we wonder what God is doing, and trying to figure God out, we lose Him. Was this God's divine joke, filling Leopold with a desire to bring the Word of God to foreign lands as a missionary, only to make his mission a tiny confessional? Always above all, obedient, Father Leopold, as with the Saints before and after him, believed that by obeying his superiors, he was obeying God. He believed in God's omnipotence, and he staked his life on that belief! Living in the calm assurance, if God had not willed he remain in Padua, and had ordained rather that he serve in far off places, He would have so directed Leopold's superiors. He recognized God's Will in his superior's orders, and spent the rest of his life obediently, tirelessly, peacefully, and joyfully bringing God to penitents in his tiny confessional.

Father Leopold, Apostle of the Confessional

When Leopold had dreamed of the priesthood, his eyes traveled over the Adriatic Sea to far-off lands to bring the Gospel of Hope to brothers and sisters starving and thirsting for this Lord Who died for them. He was not to even travel from village to village, like Father Francis and Saint Anthony (Saint of Padua), proclaiming the Good News. He was not even called to prepare others for this mission, by founding institutions or teaching in seminaries. Instead the Lord placed him in a tiny pulpit, a tiny room with no window to the outside world, with no air or light, freezing in the winter and sweltering in the summer.

Unlike the thrones of kings, this future Saint sat hours upon hours ministering to God's subjects in an old broken down chair that was as feeble as the body it held on its lap. A simple kneeler is still beside the rickety armchair, awaiting the contrite. Our Lord Crucified hanging on a wooden cross is above the *prie-dieu*,[2] a reminder of that God Who loved us so, He asked His Father, with His last words, to forgive us our sins. And then in this small cell looking down lovingly, on priest and penitent, there is a picture of Our Lady, the Mother of God who interceded at Cana and continues to intercede for Her children on earth with Her Beloved Son Jesus. As our Mother we can still see Her there, ready to help all seeking forgiveness, to reconcile with God the Father and Jesus Her Son.

In this tiny cell, for most of forty years, spending more than twelve hours of love per day, he waited and received thousands of penitents, streaming in without interruption, one after another to receive the Sacrament of Penance. Here there was no class distinction; the poor asked for forgiveness kneeling on the same prie-dieu as the rich; the famous turned to God for His Salvific Mercy, alongside the infamous; priests, bishops and religious confessed to Father Leopold (fifty priests the day before he died); professors lined up beside their students - all children of God seeking forgiveness.

The hardest hearts of stone were converted into hearts for Christ alone. Conversions came about through this little friar who was not eloquent, his voice at times hardly audible. His compassion transformed even those most hardened by years of unrepentant sinning; they began the long road to changing their lives, as they became convinced, through this humble messenger, that God loved them even when they were sinning. Upon discovering this unconditional love of the Lord, a love they had never known, true healing came about; they received the fullness of the compassionate gift of Reconciliation, and then the Life-eternal Gift of Our Lord truly Present in the Sacrament of the Eucharist.

---

[2]kneeler

Oh, if only our priests would *remember* how great is the gift they have received, the gift of administering the Sacraments to the faithful! If only we, the Mystical Body of Christ, *knew* the priceless treasures Jesus left us, those Seven Sacraments we receive through the consecrated hands of these Ambassadors of Christ, then we truly would be *one* as Jesus prayed to the Father.[3]

Faith! Have Faith!

It was his unshakable faith that brought him through years of pain and suffering. We write in one sentence, he was exiled during World War I, interned in an internment camp. It was a prison filled with other political prisoners and etc., he was a priest! He was tossed from place to place for over nineteen years, not knowing where his next assignment would bring him. It was his unconditional faith in the unconditional love of the Father, and his belief in that love which reinforced his faith! When Leopold was asked to pray for healing of mind, body or spirit, he always exclaimed: *"Faith! Have Faith! God is both Doctor and Medicine!"* But this faith was passed on to others, more by who he was than by what he said, by the light of faith that shined through him, the peace and joy, that never-ending patience toward sinners.

Father Leopold had a balance in his life. As he considered himself a terrible sinner, he feared the God of Justice; but believing in the Infinite Mercy of God, he was comforted by the consoling truth that God died for his sins. Regarding himself the worst of *sinners*, he confessed daily to remove the slightest trace of sin on his soul, so great was his fear of going to hell. When he meditated on the Mercy of God of which he spoke to penitents, it gave him peace and hope that God would forgive him, "the worst of sinners." This struggle he had with his own soul and its salvation, always seeking to please God, and always seeing himself wanting in holiness, helped him to be more compassionate and understanding of penitents who came to him

---

[3] *cf* Jn 17:20-23

needing help making a good confession.

Saint Leopold, vessel of forgiveness and wisdom

We spoke of Father Leopold's patience and charity in the confessional; we need also to write here that he was also a no-nonsense priest and confessor. If penitents came to him, trying to justify their sins, he sent them away, telling them they were not truly contrite for their sins, therefore he could not absolve them. He told them to go away and take time to prepare their confession before returning to the confessional (Reminds us of another Capuchin, Padre Pio). If a penitent was truly sorry, Father Leopold had all the time in the world to hear his sins, but to those who wanted Leopold to help them justify their actions, he told them, they were going to the wrong confessor. This was a Sacrament and as such should be treated reverently, as you would Jesus Himself, He Who left it to us.

One day, a man impatiently shoved his way past other penitents waiting on line to confess; he had no time for such nonsense; his time was too valuable! The others waiting, allowed him to go to the front of the line. When he entered the confessional, it was obvious to Father Leopold that this man had nothing to confess, that he was solely pretending to confess, in an attempt at impressing the mistress who owned the land he worked on, that he was holy and she should not evict him off her land. But after having spent a half hour in the confessional, with Father Leopold, the man departed crying.

God was Leopold's life! If his mind wandered from his Lord, even for a moment, he would confess his sin and beg the Lord for forgiveness. He said, *"We work with our bodies here on earth, but our souls should always be in the presence of God."* One time, he was talking to someone, when suddenly he looked at the time on the clock. He cried out, *"Where has the time gone?"* He rushed to the Tabernacle to beg God's forgiveness for the few minutes he had allowed his thoughts to drift from God's presence. Does this sound harsh? Think about it, if we were in the presence of God, how would we act, how would we want

God to see us behave toward ourselves and our brothers and sisters? Would this not alter our attitudes toward all God's creation, being in His presence, using His Eyes to see with and His Ears to hear with, His Words to touch others, His Heart to love others as He loves?

Father Leopold's love for Our Blessed Mother

After Jesus, Father Leopold loved his Blessed Mother best. Like a young school boy, he brought fresh flowers to his Lady every day, placing them in front of her statue in the confessional (where flowers can be seen, till today). When he spoke of her, he was transformed into a young knight in her court. When penitents came asking him to pray for them, whether for healings from physical or spiritual illnesses, he always turned them over to Our Lady. At times, he would send them to pray before the image of Our Lady in the Basilica of St. Justina, directing them to pray, *"Blessed Lady, thy servant Father Leopold has sent me; grant me the favor I ask!"* And Our Lady often seeing the trust and moved by the confidence of these Her children, interceded on their behalf, and Her Son granted their petitions.

He never focused on himself, always turning God's children to Mother Mary or Jesus. One day, a man came to Father Leopold. He was desperate! His niece had meningitis and was near death. Father Leopold asked a servant to bring him an apple. Blessing the apple, he commanded the man to give it to his niece to eat, promising Our Lady would cure her. Upon arriving at his niece's home, he found her staring at a picture of the Blessed Mother. He handed her the apple. She began to bite huge chunks out of it, consuming it ravenously and suddenly she exclaimed she was cured! The man returned to Father Leopold. Upon hearing the good news, raising his eyes to His Mother in Heaven, he cried out, *"It was Our Lady! Oh, Blessed Virgin, how good she is!"*

One time, a man confessed to Father that he had not been to the Sacraments in years. Father Leopold gave the penitent the

Left:
*St. Leopold
Mandic went on a
Pilgrimage to
Lourdes in 1934*

Right:
*Incorrupt hand of
St. Leopold Mandic at
the Capuchin Friary in Padua, Italy*

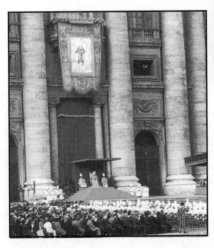

Left:
*Canonization ceremony
St. Peter's Basilica
On October 16, 1983,
he was declared St. Leopold
by Pope John Paul II*

penance, *"Recite the Salve Regina!"* He protested he no longer remembered the words. But his arguments fell on deaf ears. Father insisted the man recite the Salve Regina. Confused, the man knelt before the image of Our Lady at her altar. As he prayed, begging Our Lady for her help, suddenly he heard a sweet voice, unlike any he had ever heard, intoning the words of the Salve Regina; whereupon he joined in following Our Lady's lead. It became obvious to the man that Our Lady had completed what Her little follower had begun in his heart and soul. Needless to say this man returned to the Church; His Blessed Mother (as she is doing with so many today), had touched him and he was back, never to leave the Sacraments, again.

Our Lady saves her son from death

We are now in the year 1934; our little priest is 68 years old. He was returning from Lourdes where Our Lady had bestowed countless gifts upon him. Upon arriving at the train station in Padua, he and the parish priest of Cornegliana stepped into a carriage which was to take them to the Friary. As they turned the corner unto the Via Dante, the carriage abruptly came upon a street trolley which consisted of several trains. Now, the tracks upon which the trolley traveled placed the trolleys too close to the wall for the carriage to pass through. Onlookers shouted to the coachman to stop! But the horse, thoroughly rattled by the sudden appearance of the trolley cars, panicked and bolted, pulling the carriage carrying Father Leopold and his friend through an opening far too narrow for the carriage to pass through. The trolley came to a screeching halt and the coachman was finally able to stop the horse and carriage. Those who had witnessed the entire scene, from beginning to end, could not believe their eyes; there was not even a scratch on the carriage. The coachman testified that at the moment the horse lunged forward, the wall appeared to move back allowing the carriage to pass through, unscathed. When the onlookers recognized Father Leopold in the carriage, they exclaimed, *"No wonder! There couldn't have been an accident, not with Father in the carriage!"*

To which Father protested, *"No, that is not it! It was Our Lady who saved us. We are just back from Lourdes; it was Our Lady!"*

Father Leopold, image of Humility

"Humility personified, always ready to slip into the background,"[4] Father Leopold never focused on himself. Rather, when anyone tried to accredit favors received to him, he always pointed to the Lord and His Most Blessed Mother. When anyone leveled praise at him for the many virtues and blessings that came from him in the confessional, he humbly insisted if God had given the gifts to others, which He had bestowed on him, they would have used them far better than he.

When the faithful flocked to his confessional, not wanting them to focus on him, but rather on God and His answer to faith, he would say, *"They come with such faith that Our Lord hears them. How do I come into it?"*[5]

If he overheard someone speaking of the graces received because of his devotion to the confessional, he would simply point to the crucifix and say, *"It was He Who died for souls, not we! We are only poor men, only sinners. Only of sin are we the real authors!"*

Another time answering what he considered unwarranted praise, he insisted, *"We have always to ask for pardon, even for the good which, by God's Grace, we do; we introduce so many blemishes into His Work. We spoil the works of the Lord. We are like rotting casks, which ruin even the good wine with which they are filled."*

One day, some young ruffians, with nothing better to do, decided to pick on the little friar. They began tossing stones into the cowl which drooped down the back of his Franciscan habit. They formed a tight circle around him. Loudly taunting him in a sing-song chant they began dancing around him in a maypole

---

[4] from *Leopold Mandic, Saint of Reconciliation* by P.E. Bernardi
[5] from *Leopold Mandic, Saint of Reconciliation* by P.E. Bernardi

spirit, calling him cruel names, making fun of his size. As the stones started to pull the cowl tightly around his neck almost choking him, their laughter grew into a roar. A friend of Father Leopold coming upon the disgraceful scene, began chastising the boys for their totally unchristian behavior. Father Leopold smiled gently, and placing a restraining hand on his friend's arm, he pleaded good-naturedly, *"Let them be. Let them amuse themselves. I deserve much worse."* Are these not the words St. Francis might have said? As we study Father Leopold, we find he is so like his founder Francis who was so like his Master, Our Lord Jesus Christ.

Father Leopold - Reconciler of Christian Churches

As Father came from a country torn asunder by strife and division, caused by the fragmentation of the One True Cross, with Christians killing Christians, and knowing that peace can only come when all are one under the Chair of Peter, his lifelong vow was for the unification of all the Orthodox Churches with the Roman Catholic Church.[6] And this vow he took every day of his life, offering all his fasting, prayer and suffering up to Our Heavenly Father, supplicating Him to bring about this unity His Son had prayed for.

Our little Saint had prayed to go to the Orient, with his fellow Franciscans as a Missionary; his mission to bring Orthodox brothers and sisters back home to the One True Church. Because of his poor health, his superiors would not grant permission. But a wise friend had a suggestion which Father Leopold followed faithfully all the years of his priesthood: *"Dear Father, you really cannot go to the Orient; try to convince yourself. But you can regard your work as the Orient and work with that aim."* Father Leopold that day made a solemn commitment, *"Every soul which comes to me and asks for my*

---

[6] Read more about this tragic split and how it came about in Bob and Penny Lord's book: *Scandal of the Cross and Its Triumph, Heresies throughout the History of the Church*, in their chapter on The Greek Schism.

humble service will be, for the time being, my Orient."

When a penitent came into the confessional, with the eyes of his heart, Father Leopold saw not only him; before him, he saw the penitent accompanied by an *"oriental dissident, whom only God knew."* Father conceived his mission in the confessional, as a means of sowing seeds which God could make blossom, far, far away. When Father ministered the Sacrament of Reconciliation, he confessed the penitent with all the passion and zeal he could muster, never too tired or sick. He saw himself as *"a little bird in a cage, his heart over the sea* (in the Orient),*"* always trusting in the Holy Spirit Who is not confined to time, space or distance, but can do all things in His timetable. He lived for the hope that in his humble confessional, he could in his small way reconcile the members of the different Christian Churches. This is why he is known, not only as the Saint of Reconciliation of Sinners, but of Christian Churches.

September 23, 1927, Father Leopold made the following vows in the house of the Society of Jesus in Padua:

"I Father Leopold Mandic Zaravic, believe and think that the most Blessed Virgin Mary, the co-redeemer of mankind, is the moral grace, since all of us have received from her plenitude; therefore, according to the nature of my ministry, in order to accomplish its mission towards the Oriental peoples in that part which according to my ministry can be accomplished by me, I vow to commit all my life's strength, in every moment, with every solicitude, in the way I have intended, for the return of the Oriental dissidents to the Catholic Unity."

Dedicated to this vow, he barely slept five hours, rising well before the other friars, preparing for the Mass and then when it was over, rushing to the confessional where penitents were already awaiting him. He left the tiny cell where he heard confessions (serving 12-15 hours every day) only to say Mass or to eat a very small portion of food. His day at an end, he knelt and prayed well into the night for penitents and dissidents alike.

His mission completed for that day, then with the accompaniment of the Angels, he proceeded to fall into a peace-filled sleep.

There were times, he had just retired, when he heard the confessional bell or a brother friar knock on his door asking to go to confession; he quickly rose and entered the confessional, granting the penitent the same attention and compassion he would have, had he had a full night's sleep. Neither high fevers nor extreme fatigue could keep him from greeting and serving his fellow man cheerfully, each one a precious soul to be saved.

A few days before he died, knowing he was close to going to the Father, he shared that although he had been hearing confessions for over fifty years, his conscience did not trouble him for being so willing to readily grant absolutions; but instead that he grieved for the few times he had not been able to, accusing himself of not having done possibly all he could to make it come about, crying, possibly if he had taken more time! We see here the Heart of Jesus Who when He told Judas to be quick about it, desired he repent and be saved. But studying about Heaven, Hell and Purgatory, we know that God loves us so, He will allow us to go even to Hell.[7] When he was accused of being too lenient with sinners, he would point to Jesus on the Cross, saying *"Look at Him, how much He loved sinners. He died for us. What I do is nothing!"*

God granted many gifts to this little hidden away Saint

God bestowed upon Leopold the gift of wisdom and the gift of compassion. When he heard confession, he would often cry with the penitent, saying, *"You see, here we are two sinners who need God's forgiveness. Throw out! Throw out the evil in you. Then you will feel much better."* They loved him! No one could resist him; not even the most hardened sinner. He loved all the souls who came before him, knowing that Jesus loved them first, right up to the Cross.

---

[7]Read more about this in Bob and Penny Lord's book *Visions of Heaven, Hell and Purgatory*

If a penitent seemed reluctant to go to confession, he would scold gently, *"Do you believe in Christ? And do you believe that the confessor speaks on His behalf? Then obey! I obey my confessor."* Although his words were strong, his heart revealed the great love he felt for this soul before him, and the penitent confessed, tears streaming down his eyes. [Do we realize the priest in the confessional represents *Christ* and it is the priest in the *Person of Christ* who forgives, because Jesus pre-ordained him to do so, as one of the last acts He performed on earth? Do we believe?]

Father Leopold had the Gift of Prophecy

Father would foretell a happening in such a simple, modest manner no one paid much attention, except when it came about, and they remembered he had foretold its occurrence.

One time, after a young woman had finished confessing to him, he called her into the sacristy; his face surrounded by a white light, he told her that God had great plans for her, and to be faithful to Him. This young woman many years later founded the Handmaids of the Holy Trinity. But when she had confessed years before, she had nothing remotely resembling this in mind.

Another time, on March 18th, the vigil of St. Joseph, a father came to Father Leopold, desperate, his daughter was dying. Father told him to go home, that there was nothing to fear; tomorrow was the Feast of St. Joseph and he would intercede with Jesus and she would be cured. Six o'clock the following morning Father celebrated Mass and the young girl was instantly cured, to the joy, awe and wonder of her whole family. When the father returned to Father Leopold to thank him, he said, *"It was Saint Joseph; thank him. Didn't I tell you St. Joseph could do wonderful things?"* Again, as with all the Saints, what do we see? Humility and the desire to decrease while God increases.

Father Leopold foretold the war and devastation that would overcome Italy in the Second World War. One day, when a friend visited Father, he noticed he had been crying. He asked him why! Father said he had had a dream where he saw Italy drowning in a sea of blood and flames. When he finished telling his dream, he covered his face and began crying once again, pleading with God he be wrong. After a few minutes, he uncovered his face and pulling himself upright, he sorrowfully proclaimed he was not wrong, indeed Italy would be covered in blood and flames. Father's prophecy was to sadly come to pass when the Nazis invaded Italy raping and killing women and their children before their eyes, razing homes and churches indiscriminately.

War had come to Italy and the ravages of war were striking city after city, bombs flying through the air, missing their intended strike and leveling the homes of the innocent as well as God's holy houses, the churches. When Father Leopold was asked if Padua would be bombed and the Capuchin monastery as well, with a heavy heart he predicted, *"Padua will be hit heavily! The friary and the church will be hit, too, but this little cell (referring to his confessional) no, this no! God has shown such great mercy here to so many souls that it must remain as a monument to His Kindness."*

[This reminds us of Mother Angelica's miraculous healing, where after more than forty-four years she threw aside her crutches and body brace and walked unaided. When she spoke of her miraculous cure, like the Saints before her, rather than focusing on herself, she pointed to this as a gift to God's people, a sign of hope, a monument to God's love which has no limits, no boundaries.]

During an air raid, May 14, 1944, planes were heard flying over Padua and their worst fear came to pass, bombs fell from the sky, scattering menacingly over the city; the church and friary were hit by five massive bombs which were designed to explode, disseminating its devastation in broken jagged pieces over a wide area, creating total destruction to everything within its path. Devastate they did, and their mission to destroy everything in their wake was accomplished, *except* for the statue of the Blessed

Mother and the little confessional-cell where God the Father had shown so much mercy on His children through his tiny vessel, Father Leopold.

Father could read men's hearts! He could read a penitent's soul like an open book. There were times, he would say, *"Stop I know everything,"* and then to let the penitent know he did, Father would tell him his sins. A young Capuchin desiring to make a general confession, before taking his solemn vows, no sooner began confessing his sins, when Father Leopold told him to stop; assuring him he knew the rest. When the student begged to finish, lest there be any sins remaining on his soul, Father began recounting for close to twenty minutes all the young friar's sins, adding things that even the young man had forgotten when he was making a thorough examination of conscience. Seeing he was at last at peace, Father Leopold told him, *"See, it was not necessary for you to accuse yourself. I knew everything! Learn to believe the word of the confessor."*

Father Leopold prepares to go Home

Like Don Bosco, life was now quickly ebbing out of the little confessor. He started to go down hill after his Golden Jubilee, September 22, 1940. He had always suffered with pains in his stomach, but the winter of 1941 found him with such acute pains, he could not longer hide them. He was no longer able to eat; his strength was gone; but the physical pain was nothing compared to the spiritual pain he was made to endure. Father Leopold no longer could hear confessions, his health was so seriously impaired, he was confined to his bed. He bore his afflictions so quietly, no one knew how quickly he was climbing the way to his final Calvary.

The doctors did not believe he would survive the winter, but then spring came and our little troubadour of compassion seemed to rally, enough to return to his *little cell*. But those who came left crying; it was obvious only his deep love kept him going. Life was betraying his spirit. Winter came and with it his decline. By spring of 1942, he was at last sharing he felt like he had no strength left.

The pains in his stomach became so excruciating, he was forced to remain in bed. And so, on March 25, 1942, Father Leopold received the Last Rites of the Church. He was later brought to the hospital where he received a blood transfusion, from which he appeared to rally for a brief time. His friends and the friars continued to gather around his bed fearing he would leave them any time. But Leopold was not finished serving. From his sick bed, about to meet His Divine Savior, he continued to hear confessions.

He returned to the friary and he looked forward to resuming his apostolate to sinners, but God had another plan. The doctors discovered a tumor in his esophagus, and he could no longer swallow food of any kind. The only nourishment he could swallow was his Lord in the Holy Eucharist. Jesus had shared so many gifts with him, He would now share His Passion; the physical and spiritual pain ascended as he ascended closer and closer to his cross. As with Jesus, he found his consolation in the Blessed Mother. He wrote: *"I have so much need that the august Lady deign to have pity on me. I want to hope in Her even when She has to reject my prayers. She is my Mother; that is enough for me."* Our Lady was there to carry Her little son through his last struggle in life and was now waiting to take him to Heaven.

Father Leopold had always asked the Lord to have him *"die in harness,"* and the Lord obliged him. In the infirmary, near death, he never stopped hearing confessions. He continued throughout his last day. Although one could see him struggling for each breath, he tirelessly fulfilled his ministry till the end, hearing among others the confessions of fifty priests the day before he died.

The Saint is dead; long live our Saint!

The 30th of July, Father Leopold rose at 5:30 a.m. and was carried into the infirmary. He began, as he did all days, with an hour praying, preparing for the Mass. He walked slowly into the sacristy to vest up for Mass. Overtaken by a strong spasm, he fell to the ground and had to be carried to bed. For a moment, he looked as if he was going to beat death once more, when he was felled by another attack. A fellow priest came and anointed him. Our little soldier of Christ had all his faculties. He joined in with his Superior as he intoned the Hail Mary three times and the Hail Holy Queen. His voice got weaker and weaker, till after he spoke these words to his Mother the last time, *"O clement, O loving, O sweet Virgin Mary!"* his soul soared to his Heavenly Family whom he had so faithfully served on earth. His face was serene, an angelic smile on his face. Whom did you see, dear confessor? Were Our Lord and His Mother Mary waiting, with a cortege of Heavenly Angels to take you Home?

The news quickly spread, *"Our Saint is dead! Our Saint is dead!"* And they came, more than 25,000 came to say their last farewell to their confessor. The funeral was more, a triumphant procession. Their hearts were broken, for Leopold had been a confessor, a friend, a brother. His life had been to love and to have God known, so that He would be loved, and he had lived his life well. Soon letters of condolence and loss arrived from far-reaching cities of Italy, people from every walk of life, as in his confessional, rich and poor alike, saints and sinners, all sending their friend off with love.

The faithful proclaimed him a Saint long before the Church did, as they have often done. They started to visit his tomb when he was still in the cemetery in Padua. In 1963, when they investigated his remains, they found his body incorrupt, and at that time moved it to a special chapel next to the Confessional-cell where he spent most his fifty years of priesthood. As he had prophesied, the cell is there till today, a sign of God's everlasting mercy and love.

The many times we have gone to this shrine, to study our Saint for this book and the television program we made for EWTN, we have always seen devotees of this Saint praying at his tomb. Although you will meet people speaking many tongues, from many walks of life, the thing that most impressed us was the faithful from that area, from busy industrial, university-sophisticated Padua coming at all hours of the day to visit and ask their confessor for help. There are over 3 million signatures of people who have visited and venerated our Leopold, a tiny man in stature but a giant in the Eyes of God.

A few short years after his death, prayer cards were printed in approximately 30 languages with the title: *"Novena to the Holy Trinity to obtain grace and glorification for the Servant of God, Leopold of Castelnovo, Capuchin."*

Banner flying high! St. Peter's Square filled with the faithful, Pope Paul VI, a Pope whose heart's desire was the unification of the Orthodox and the Roman Catholic Churches, on May 2, 1976 (34 years after Leopold's death) proclaimed the Church had a new Blessed - Father Leopold was now Blessed Leopold.

Another Pope visited the tomb of Blessed Leopold September the 12th, 1982 and added his signature to the other 3,000,000 signatures of faithful who have visited this shrine. On October 16th, 1983, the fifth anniversary of his Pontificate and the twenty-fifth anniversary of his Episcopate,[8] Pope John Paul II, another son of the Church from the East, declared to all the world that the Church had a new Saint - Saint Leopold!

I wish we had room to place all the miracles attributed to the intervention of this little *grand* Saint; the walls at his Shrine are lined with them; but space and time does not dictate we do so. Besides, Saint Leopold would have said, *Why all this fuss? After all, I did nothing. It was the Lord and His Mother, you know."*

---

[8]having been ordained bishop

Left:
St. Angela Merici,
*"I want to become a Saint,
because I love Jesus."*

Below: *St. Angela Merici
Pilgrim on a Journey of Faith*

Above: *Vision of St. Angela
Merici. She saw a
procession of a splendid
celestial company of Angels
and Virgins, descending
two by two from Heaven.*

St. Angela Merici

"I want to become a Saint, because I love Jesus."

The Church was in crisis! The Good Shepherd would not leave His lambs *alone* to be devoured by wolves; so once again God raised up Saints and other powerful men and women to save His Church.

In the Fourteenth Century, God wanted the Papacy to return to Rome. He knew what was going to come to pass; the Papacy had to be located in the eye of the storm, to combat the forces of dissension which were bubbling beneath the surface, and those which would erupt in the Fifteenth Century and explode in the Sixteenth. God putting his chess pieces in place, raised up a woman, St. Catherine of Siena;[1] He groomed her for her mission and when it was time, sent her to Avignon to bring the Papacy back to Rome.

But as God was maneuvering, putting His troops on the front line, the *enemy*, in an attempt to outmaneuver God, attacked the Church from the rear, initiating the birth of the Renaissance! The people were battle weary and Dark Ages depressed; they were ripe for anyone selling them something or *someone* who would bring some joy and happiness into their lives; but sadly even good things that are not holy will eventually, like a dog with a cruel master, turn on you and bite you. The Renaissance, the period of enlightenment which was to lead them out of the darkness of the Dark Ages, only led them into deeper darkness through a tunnel to hell.

In the mid 1400s Renaissance[2] had been wildly spreading its humanistic, paganistic secularism, selling man on wanting more, but not more God, more self-gratification. God seeing His

---

[1]Read more about Catherine of Siena in Bob and Penny Lord's book: *Saints and other Powerful Women in the Church.*

[2]for more on Renaissance and its effects on the Church and the world, read Bob and Penny Lord's book: *Scandal of the Cross and Its Triumph, Heresies throughout the History of the Church.*

children about to be run over by trojan horses bearing poisoned sweets called forth Saints like St. Bernardine, St. John Capistrano, and others, His plan - to offset with holiness, the evil with which the devil was unscrupulously tipping the scales.

Much of Italy had been conquered by a tyrant called Visconti who was swallowing up province after province, conquering citizens and land by intimidation, crushing their spirits by bondage and servitude, enslaving them into complete subjugation by imposing the worst forms of terrifying tyranny upon them. He trampled the forces in the North, almost effortlessly. But, as he traveled southward, ready to strike the Tuscany region, Visconti found formidable fighters, free spirits, people of fire and focus who would not be enslaved! Although under the Medicis, this would not have been called a democratic form of government, it was Tuscany for and by Tuscans.

The Fifteenth Century no better than the Fourteenth, God, countering evil with good, raised up a unique Saint. Permissiveness and promiscuity were running wild like the wine and revelry of the times, God raised a Saint who will not only be a contradiction in this hedonistic society, she will gather others to follow her in her divine quest to live a life of holiness. And so through her, a new heretofore unknown charism will be born into this troubled time, through another Saint who was willing *"to do the ridiculous so that God would be moved to do the miraculous."*[3]

The Fifteenth Century is here; the Church needs a Saint!

We are in the north of Italy, in a little village called Desenzano, east of Brescia. The quiet little town lies peacefully on picturesque Lake Garda, on the outskirts of the Lombardy region. If your eye travels northward on the map, you will see the village of Trent where the Council of Trent was held in the Sixteenth Century, in 1545, five years after our Saint died. We never know what our actions are going to bring about; but one

---

[3] a quotation from Mother Angelica

thing we can be sure, they will either be life-giving or life-ending. This is the story of a woman who will contribute to the *life* of her Church, the Church which Jesus founded, our beloved Roman Catholic Church.

"I want to become a Saint because I love Jesus!"

One chilly damp Spring morning, March 21, 1474, to be exact, a child was born, a girl to a farmer named Giovanni, and his wife Signora Merici, who was of the noble family - the Biancosi of Salo. From the very beginning, the child Angela was wrapped in a robe of piety and holiness, her parents having one focus, to bring her up to love and serve Jesus. And they did, first by who they were, then by word and deed. Angela asked her father to read to her, so that she could learn about the Saints and Virgin Martyrs of the past. Together they delved into the Bible, and other spiritual books pouring over stories of those who shaped the Church. Each evening after chores were over, they would sit by the fire and travel with those who lived and died for Mother Church.

Soon this child, all of five years old, began living a contemplative life, fasting and performing acts of mortification. She was not, however a sad, somber girl; everyone in the village loved her and looked forward to this little bundle of energy and joy stopping to say hello to them. They would always send a little something home with her which she would share with her family. When the bells would toll from the parish church nearby, summoning them to pray the Angelus, and her family was in the middle of feeding the chickens, her parents would instruct their children to kneel down and tell the Lord they were heartily sorry they could not come to His altar at that time, but that they were offering all their work, feeding His little creatures, to Him; then they should end by pleading with the Lord to accept this labor as their prayer. Her parents were honest, pious people who, although poor in the eyes of the world, were rich with super abundant graces from Heaven.

Angela's childhood comes to an end!

Angela grew up a happy child, following her parents wherever they went. Like her father, she told her siblings and other children stories of Our Lady. A favorite was the story of Our Lady of Siracusa. She loved to tell stories of such Saints as St. Tarcisius, the little acolyte who died defending the Eucharist.[4] Life was so good; Angela was so happy! But that was soon to end.

One day her father was robust and virile, a strong man who rarely had a sick day in his life, and then one day he was gravely ill! All at once he was helpless to withstand whatever was robbing him of life on earth. After days of doing everything of a scientific as well as spiritual nature to save him, he was dying. Angela held her father's hand, consoling him, speaking to him of the Jesus, Mary and Joseph he so often spoke of, how They would all be there to take him Home. Angela saw her father die a peaceful, resigned death, his lips and eyes nailed to the Crucified Lord on the Cross. Her spirit was at rest because she knew the Lord would not wait long till her father was with Him; but she would miss him; their time together went too fast.

Life became almost bearable, time healing somewhat the wounds of her father's passing, when Angela was to suffer another loss, the death of her older sister! She had been more than a *physical* sister - she was her spiritual sister, sharing in her spiritual walk, understanding and affirming her. Her inconsolable grief, at losing the one closest to her, this sister who was so like her in mind and heart, was further compounded by the knowledge her sister had died without having received the Last Sacraments. Not even the parish priest's confidence that since her sister had lived a most holy, angelic life, Angela could be assured she was with the Lord, was enough to convince Angela that her sister went to Heaven. None of the efforts made by her mother to

---

[4]For more about this brave altar boy, read Bob and Penny's book: *This is My Body, This is My Blood, Miracles of the Eucharist, Book I*

reassure her, consoled her; nothing eased the heartache Angela felt, her young heart bleeding out of fear, wondering where her sister was. She could neither eat nor sleep. She prayed throughout the night, *"Please Lord, tell me if my sister is united with You in Heaven."*

Then one day at twelve o'clock, the noon hour, the church bell began tolling, it was time for the Angelus. As Angela was praying, sharing her pain with Jesus, a luminous light suddenly filled the sky and before her, was a company of Angels surrounding her sister, escorting her to Heaven. As she beheld her, she could see her loving sister tranquil and peaceful, her eyes fixed on things *Above*, ascending, no, gliding along with her Heavenly Guides toward her Lord and Savior. The Lord, in His mercy had granted Angela her first vision! She would have many in her lifetime, but none would surpass this vision which reassured her beyond any doubt that her dear sister was in Heaven with her Lord Jesus. Till the day she died she could vividly paint (with words) the picture she had seen!

As the noble families of the village considered Angela well-bred, her mother being of noble birth, and considering her family was impoverished as a result of falling into hard times, and what with Angela's fine breeding and deep spirituality, they began to take notice of Angela. Angela was growing in beauty, and the young men of these fine families soon became very attracted to her. They began to ask her mother for Angela's hand in marriage.

It was time for Angela to tell her mother that the day she had had a vision of her sister ascending to Heaven, she pledged her troth to Jesus to be His bride then and forever. Having done so, she could not consider any earthly spouse. Her mother, remembering how this child of hers was spiritual from her earliest years, did not pursue the question of Angela considering the proposals of marriage tendered by the fairest sons of the fairest families. She recognized she was not fighting Angela but the One Who had chosen her for His own.

Soon after, her mother passed out on the kitchen floor; thank God there had been a farmer's wife with her; she called for help and they placed Angela's mother in bed. *Angela was eighteen years old.* Knowing her time was growing short, her mother called Angela into her bedroom. She blessed her and thanked her for all the consolation and strength she had always given her. She told her that now Jesus, Angela's Spouse, would have to be her sole consolation, as she was leaving Angela to join her husband and daughter in Heaven. She told her to give a message to her brother, Angela's uncle, that she had died in peace and he must promise to take Angela into his family as his very own. That evening, after receiving the Last Rites of the Church, her mother closed her eyes forever. Angela was alone!

Angela said nothing; it was as if she were walking in her sleep. Her Uncle Biancosi came and buried his sister next to her husband and daughter. Angela, her eyes filled with tears, said goodby to Father, Mother and Sister. It was that terrible time after a funeral when all there is, is goodby, goodby to all you have known, and a painful hello to the frightful unknown. But for Biancosi, to fulfill his sister's dying wishes would not be difficult; Angela was lovable. Angela was given a second family!

Life would never be the same! Angela began life with her uncle in the village of Salo. Whereas life in Desenzano with its poverty was joyful, with its providential but sparse gifts from God, life in Salo with all its sumptuous surroundings and luxury, was painful; for she had long ago decided her life was to be one of austerity like that of St. Francis.[5]

Through no fault of her own, Angela *again* gained the attention of the fine families and their sons, *now* of Salo. But Angela, her heart already owned by the Lord, asked her uncle if she could visit the Carmelite Convent, which her mother had spoken of with so much love and fond memories. There, in the chapel, while praying before the statue of Our Lady of Mt.

---

[5]St. Francis of Assisi died almost 250 years before she was born

Carmel, she saw a sweet image of the Virgin Mother who told her to prostrate herself before her Son and begin a new life with Him. Mother Mary shared how from the moment she said yes to the Angel Gabriel, to the moment her beloved Son breathed His last on the Cross, she lived for Him, and then thereafter. She asked Angela, *"Can you do likewise?"* Mother Mary told Angela, as she had lost her earthly mother, She, Mary would be her Heavenly Mother; She would guide her in her walk toward Jesus and eternal life with Him. But she warned her to be the bride of Jesus is to be the bride of the *Crucified* Lord, to willingly suffer with Him, beside her at the foot of the Cross.

Angela's uncle continued to introduce her to the finest families, who all fell in love with her and her goodness. Although she was civil and kind, her heart had been given to the Supreme Lover of the Universe and she was eternally bonded to Him. She followed the same austere walk of life she had walked in Desenzano as a child; but now an adult, she was even stricter in her lessons and spiritual exercises. First thing in the morning she would go to the nearby church of St. Bernardino of the Friars Minor Observants and attend Mass, participating in every part of the Holy Sacrifice, to the degree she was allowed. As the Mass progressed, her heart would begin to swell. As the priest came closer and closer to that great moment when he would lift high the Host, her Jesus Present for all to see, who have eyes to see, she thought, *"Oh, if only I could die right now and be with You, adoring You in Your Beatific Vision."*

Angela also found Jesus in the pots and pans.[6] Angela helped her aunt cook, kneed the bread, fetch water from the well, all and everything that was asked of her with joy and peaceful resignation.

But her life was not only filled with peace and tranquility. Although dedicated to an austere life, she faced temptations like any girl her age. One night, she heard a young man serenading a

---

[6]like Saint Teresa of Avila

Above: *St. Angela Merici with the Company of Virgins*

Left: *St. Angela Merici*
Statue of the Saint in the Piazza
Malvezzi in Desenzano, Italy

Above: *Incorrupt body of St.*
Angela Merici at her Shrine in
Brescia, Italy

young girl outside her window. It was so sweet, so romantic. She prayed all the harder, asking the Lord to forgive her for her thoughts, her temptations; she loved Him and wanted Him alone! Now, here was this sweet innocent girl who had pledged her faithfulness to the Lord and He was allowing her to suffer this temptation.

Suddenly, if that was not enough, who should appear, one of the most handsome young men she had ever seen. He looked like an Angel! He was perfect! But there was something about his eyes; they were not gentle like a celestial Angel; they were more like some of the men she had met; no, he was the fallen angel who had seduced Eve in the garden of Eden. Angela cried out, *"Return to the inferno of hell, enemy of the Cross! I recognize you; you are not an Angel of God."* The vision disappeared and she lay there prostrate, her face on the ground. Although relieved he had left, she was trembling, knowing she had faced the king of darkness, and too prudent to think that was the end of it.

There was a battle being waged between the good Angels and the fallen ones in Italy which spread to the province of Lombardy and then filtered down to the little village of Salo, with her uncle's children, as well as other youths, the spoils. As she was preparing for her consecrated religious life with Jesus, praying in her little room, she could sense a turbulence, a troubled spirit. News came to her uncle's home that there were orgies scheduled for the young, to take place at the lake, going as far as the citizens of Salo would permit! Under the guise it was a civil and religious celebration, it would be complete with food, music and revelry, more like debauchery.

In addition, the young members of the Casa Biancosi were talking about another blasphemy planned for the Second Sunday after Easter, when the entire town would be celebrating the Feast Day of St. Lawrence. Multitudes of men and women were to break into the festivities, desecrating the holiness of the Feast Day and time of year, by all kinds of scandalous behavior. Some evil men from the village, to further disturb the sanctity of the Feast, invited mercenaries, in the company of loose women, to come and parade through the town, behaving like the ancient Romans who reveled in the streets of decadent Rome, honoring the Roman and Greek god of wine and revelry, Bacchus. The plan was to end this bacchanalian march with all sorts of perverted, indecent acts performed on the altar in the church.

But God always balancing the odds, placed a band of Franciscan friars in a convent nearby, to serve at the Church of Saint Mary. They were well received and respected, like a breath of fresh air in an area that was becoming polluted by the worldly influences and temptations of the forces invading this small village. Part of their duties was to lead the villagers in celebrating the Feast of St. Lawrence each year.

What did Angela do? She prayed and did penance for those who would lose their souls, and begged God to spare the young, especially those of the Biancosi household, from falling into the fires of hell that day. This would be her life, to do penance for the sins of the world. What is it that Mother Mary said to the children of Fatima, *"Many are going to hell, because so few will pray, fast and sacrifice."*

Now, Dukes and Lords from not only this village but others, from as far as Venice, frequently came to this very important Feast of St. Lawrence. Whereas the religious part of the Feast was run by the Rectors of the Friary, the secular part, that of the commune, was supervised and under the tutelage of the Duke of the village. As this was not only a religious feast, but one that the commune or local government sponsors, the sacrilegious travesties were brought to the attention of the Duke and he forbid not only the parade but the rest of the planned debauchery.

Years later, the Duke of Salo, on the 1st of April, 1548 not only banned, for all time, baccanalian parades, but to satisfy the appetites of those craving excitement, instituted a Palio,[7] to be held in honor of St. Lawrence on his Feast Day, each year. He also decreed they were not to forget, with the excitement of celebrating, eating and singing, the reason for this day was to celebrate the Feast of a Martyr who died for the Church.

Can we make a difference? How did all these proposed demonic activities come to the attention of the proper authorities? Was it through Angela's prayers and sacrifice? Well, God overcame evil, and isn't that all that counts?

Angela becomes a Franciscan Tertiary

It continued to be a sad time for Christians. What with a Borgia Pope Alexander VI, the threat of invasion by the Turkish saracens and with it the end of Christianity, Italy was being besieged and destroyed from without and within. It was time for prayer and penance. Angela knew the Lord wanted to use her, but how? She understood the times and the danger awaiting God's children and willingly offered herself as victim-soul for the salvation of the Church.

Angela was admitted into the Third Order of St. Francis as a Tertiary. Her lifestyle became even more austere. Endeavoring to be more like the Poor One of Assisi, St. Francis, she desired no bed, preferring to sleep on the floor, and subsisted on a small repast of bread, a little water and some vegetables. Shedding the fine clothes provided by her uncle and aunt, she donned the robes of St. Francis, went among the poor, tended the sick, shared what food she had, consoled the dying and the families left behind. She was a Saint in their midst, and that she was of the nobility, gave them a newfound dignity. But Angela knew it was time to leave the comfort of her uncle's home and return to Desenzano. She was about twenty-six years old by this time.

---

[7]A Palio is when the finest horses (entered by different countries) compete, with men from the districts of Tuscany, who have never been on the horses before, riding bareback.

Angela returns home to Desenzano

     She has returned to her native village of Desenzano. Now there, without family and a place to live, she wonders what she is supposed to do. Is she to enter a monastery, or what? She was both dismayed and appalled at the lack of education, she saw upon arriving there, the total ignorance which prevailed among the children of the poor! She discovered their parents wouldn't or couldn't teach them about their Faith. This ignorance would be perpetuated from one generation to the next, unless someone did something about it.

     It was harvest time, and all the farmers were gathered under the trees, in Bruduzzo, where they would *together* round up the crop. They were all eating and drinking, laughing and rejoicing because the yield looked good! But off in the distance was Angela. She chose to eat alone, as she was more hungry for the Word of God than the food of man, more focused on filling her spirit than her stomach. She was praying, entreating God to show her His Plan.

     "You sent me back here, but what am I supposed to do? Enlighten me, please Lord!" The Lord responded by filling the air with the sweetest perfume; the birds began to chirp happily in the trees; the sky opened up; the clouds disappeared; and low and behold Angela saw a procession of a splendid celestial company of Angels and Virgins, descending two by two from Heaven, processing down a regal, magnificent staircase. Angels were playing various instruments, accompanying the Virgins who were singing. Then who passed the others, coming toward Angela but her sister who had died. She looked beautiful and oh so happy. She told Angela that the Lord wanted to use her; that it was His desire she form a *Company of Virgins*, with whom the task He had planned for her would come about, and that this Company was to be formed in Brescia!

     Now, Angela preferred to join a contemplative order, and serve her Lord in the cloister, but it was obvious the Lord wanted her to be a religious in the world, serving Him through serving

His children out in the world. She discussed this with some friends, mostly other tertiaries. Now they were in the same boat she was; they had little money and less resources, but what they lacked in material assets they excelled in love and willingness to make a difference. What could they do? They rallied around her; if she would lead the way, they would follow.

Angela was a born leader. Their first step was to round up the young girls of the village and begin to teach them. Our Omnipotent God would work with humility! The action which began with one small step grew and grew, and became so successful, the band of tertiaries were asked to open other schools in other villages.

Angela has a vision; she is to found a school in Brescia!

Italy is again in dire times, the Italians divided, the French and Spaniards collaborating to pick off village after village, sharing the spoil; Angela was asked to go to Brescia. Remembering her vision in Bruduzzo, she agreed! Arriving in Brescia, Angela was soon offered a place to live. There was a noble family in Brescia whom she had once helped. Catherine Patengola had lost her two sons. All the joy that had formerly filled her sumptuous home was gone; and she, day by day, lost all desire to live. The Franciscan friars feeling helpless, turned to Angela; they asked if she would console her. Angela visited the grieving mother; she spoke softly and lovingly; she listened patiently while Catherine vented all her anger against God. Then Angela shared how desolate she had felt when she lost father, then mother, then sister, and how she did not know why God took them when He did; but one thing she knew - He loved her and He loves Catherine.

As days passed into weeks, Catherine became stronger and stronger. And so when Angela came to Brescia, Catherine not only offered her a home, through her Angela met Catherine's nephew Jerome,[8] and through him Augustine Gallo and James

---

[8]he would found the *Hospital for the Incurable* in Brescia

Chizzola.[9] A friendship began which would last a lifetime. As she spoke of the need, and possibility of bringing about change, she found them growing more and more eager to help. They contributed ideas on how she might go about forming her company, and put Angela in contact with the wealthy men and women of Brescia.

After a few months, Catherine fully recovered, and able to stand on her own two feet, Angela left her home; and with her tertiaries, moved into the home donated by Anthony Romano on the Via S. Agata[10] to better achieve her mission. The home was close to the church so the women could receive the Sacraments and attend Mass frequently, and with this central location make their ministry known to other young women.

Angela - Pilgrim on a Journey of Faith

From time to time, Angela, the contemplative, sought the quiet voice of the Lord, by making a pilgrimage to a holy Shrine. These journeys of faith influenced her life, and reinforced her conviction that she was doing the Will of God. On one occasion, she journeyed to the town of Mantua to visit the tomb of Blessed Osanna of Mantua,[11] a mystic whom Angela most admired. She returned to Brescia so inspired, she began to seek out young men, counselling them on seeking the Will of God. She spoke so powerfully, many decided to become priests. When she visited the place of her birth, Desenzano, then Salo, and finally Brescia she was more than ever determined to educate the children of the poor.

When the opportunity to visit the Holy Land presented itself, she joyfully accepted. From her youngest years, her life had been filled with the awe and wonder of God's love that she

---

[9]also involved in the future *Hospital for the Incurable* in Brescia

[10]Agatha

[11]a contemporary of St. Angela Merici, as St. Angela was born in 1474 and Bl. Osanna in 1449. She died in 1505, therefore when St. Angela visited her tomb she had not been dead long.

had discovered through reading Sacred Scripture. She had meditated on Jesus' life and death on the Cross. To think, now she would walk where her Lord walked, look upon the Sea of Galilee where He walked on water, climb the Mount of the Beatitudes where He multiplied the loaves and fishes feeding more than 5,000, stand in the Garden of Gethsemane where He sweat blood for our sins, and then kneel at Calvary where He gave up His life for her.

But her voyage was not to go exactly as planned. When they reached Crete, Angela lost her sight; she was totally blind! When her companions begged they all turn back, she insisted they continue with the Pilgrimage. As she walked along the Via Dolorosa where Jesus walked the Way of the Cross, she saw her Lord, bleeding, stumbling, falling under the weight of her sins and getting up to fall another time, out of love for her; but it was with the eyes of her heart, as she did not regain her eyesight until her boat landed in Crete, once again, at the very spot where she had first lost her eyesight. She had been praying before her Lord crucified on the Cross, tears pouring down her face, meditating on having been on the very spot where He offered up His Life to the Father for the redemption of our sins. She could not stop crying; and then it happened, her eyes opened and she could see!

She went to many holy places, but next to the Holy Land, her audience with Pope Clement VII was the highlight of her pilgrimages. In 1525, the Church was once again bleeding, with attacks being leveled at her now from Germany, through one of her own - Fr. Martin Luther. If ever there was time for a Holy Year to be proclaimed it was in the Sixteenth Century, in 1525. The Pope invited all the faithful to pilgrimage to Rome to celebrate the Holy Year and receive an indulgence. Angela was so excited, not only with the possibility of seeing the Pope, but to visit the Basilicas of Rome, the Catacombs where the Martyrs were laid to rest, the Coliseum where the blood of the Martyrs sanctified that monstrous theater of death.

To show the high regard, the Pope had for St. Angela

Merici and her work, he granted her a private audience. She knelt before him, and he blessed her. He was so enchanted by her, her enthusiasm, her knowledge, her love for the poor and most of all for Mother Church, he asked her to remain in Rome, and continue her work there. Which she did; but then Brescia and the needs of the poor there, called to her, and she was on her way back home.

Brescia is torn by Lutheranism and war!

Angela arrived in Brescia, only to see Lutheranism dividing the nobility and the Church. It was a sad time! Division causing dissension, and dissension bringing about death. *A house divided against itself will fall.* Angela would battle this Protestant revolution with education! By teaching the young the true Faith, she would stem the spread of Lutheranism in Brescia and environs.[12] She warned the populace, at large, how important it was to be vigilant, as in some parts of Italy and much of Europe the Faith was being taken from the faithful. She said, *"The devil never sleeps, but attacks in a thousand disguises, looking for your ruination. Therefore be on guard; take care. Be of one accord, believing in the One Church and the One Truth. Like the early Apostles and the early Christians be of one heart and mind. Continue to walk the straight path to God."* She said that *"The devil will appear under the guise of being good. Beware of the darkness, alone!"* How often do we hear that being said today!

In the mountains, the citizens hid from the Spaniards; the Germans were fast approaching Brescia from another front; the French had already made their inroads. The troops brought with them not only death to the body but also to the soul. *To the conquerors go the spoils!* They raped and pillaged; they broke their spirits, took away their dignity, closed their churches; no

---

[12]Read more on Luther and the attacks against the Church in Bob and Penny Lord's Trilogy: *Treasures of the Church, That which makes us Catholic; Tragedy of the Reformation; Cults, Battle of the Angels.*

one was exempt from their heartlessness. If that was not catastrophic enough, no sooner had she arrived in Brescia, the city was being attacked by Charles V, Emperor of the Holy Roman Empire, who was set on taking Brescia for himself, as part of his newly acquired Kingdom of Lombardy. It was essential all those not bearing arms, leave at once! And so Angela and her Company had to leave for Cremona where she remained until peace returned to Brescia.

Peace at last; thank God, peace at last. Angela and her companions returned to Brescia. The citizens cheered, for they looked upon Angela not only as their benefactress, because of her love and charity towards them, they venerated her as a prophetess and Saint! There were many reasons for this devotion. One day, after Holy Mass was concluded, Angela fell into a lengthy ecstasy lasting hours, during which time, she was seen levitating by many reliable witnesses.

Angela - consoler of the mighty and the poor

Angela became known as consoler of lost souls. Rich or poor, Angela saw them with the eyes of Jesus and they were all children in need. Duke Francesco II Sforza, lost Milan because the King of France coveted it for himself. He came to Brescia, and the Augustinian Hermits offered him asylum. But he found no peace! He was despondent, grieving inconsolably over the loss of his land. He would talk endlessly of how, when he was but eight years old, he had revisited his home, only to find it in ruins, how he found his father imprisoned, and then with nothing remaining he went into exile in Germany. He recounted over and over again, how, after being there for twelve years, he could no longer stand the tyranny of his older brother and with the help of the Swiss went into exile for another eight years. He cried when he shared how, when at thirty years old, he returned to Milan and his people had welcomed him with open arms. He had freed them from their invaders, only to be taken from them. How they cheered when he became Duke of Milan. Oh, how he missed them and Milan!

What he had sought from his country and from other countries, to be important among men, brought him no contentment or happiness; it was through the words of the humble Angela that he was to find peace and resignation.

Angela was a peacemaker. It was through her intervention that reconciliation came about between two very important personages in Brescia, Francesco Salo and Gianfrancesco Martinengo.

At last, the Company of Saint Ursula is formed!

"Take heart, Angela; before you die you will found at Brescia a company of maidens similar to those you have just seen." God had spoken these words, as Angela had beheld a vision of Angels and Virgins descending a staircase from Heaven. At that time she had received the command she was to form a *Company of Virgins.* As we have seen in our own lives and the life of our ministry, God tells us His Will for us, outlines His plan, but very often it is, as in the case of Angela Merici, thirty or so years before He has it come to pass. Brother Joseph says that God always speaks to us in the future tense. Angela was fifty-eight years old, when in 1533, she knew it was time to fulfill the prophecy, time to execute God's command to her.

She moved into quarters next to the Church of Sant Afra,[13] and there she brought twelve girls who would live with her in this house. She believed, it would be most conducive for the young women of the nobility and those of poor circumstances to dwell together, because they would be sustained and animated by the Lord and His Sacraments (in the church next door) fortifying them, enabling them to live the Gospel life.

There were a small group of women, who took the same vows as those living together, but lived with their parents or relatives at home. This house was also where these girls would come together with those who lived in the house and work side by side with them, pray together, and perform whatever act of

---

[13]now called *Santuario de Sant'Angela Merici*

charity they were called upon to do.

The little company became so alive in Brescia, their number grew! Twenty-eight more women consecrated themselves to the Company of St. Ursula, two short years later. The young women wore no habits, but St. Angela recommended they wear modest black dresses. They did not take vows, the sisters lived for the most part in their own homes, or if they lived together they were not cloistered and moved freely about serving the needs of the community.

Their charism was to live a holy life, whether together in the little house or with their families; they were to come together to attend classes and worship, and to fulfill any tasks assigned them. Their main apostolate was one of teaching. And the Company which still headquarters out of that same house, living the original charism of their foundress[14] and the Ursulines[15] who were later formed into an Order by Charles Borromeo, have never forgotten that this is their main charism - to teach young women, especially of the poor.

Angela Merici did not know how to write, so she had to dictate the Rule to a professor who in turn, wrote it all down. She named the Company after the young virgin Martyr, Ursula, remembering the stories her father told her of this pure victim-soul who lived a pious life dedicated to the Lord, to the point of dying rather than deny Him, by marrying the son of a pagan King. The Rule was approved in 1536 by the Vicar General of the Bishop of Brescia. In 1537, when elections were called, Angela Merici was *unanimously* elected Superior and she held that office for the last five years of her life, until she became too ill.

Angela went to bed one cold day in January, never to rise again. Days later, she said her last goodbys to her beloved

---

[14]as outlined above
[15]The Ursulines consider this day, November 25, 1535, the day Angela Merici moved her company into the little house next to the church, the date of the foundation of the Ursuline Order, although during Angela's lifetime it was more of an association.

companions and left on her last pilgrimage to kneel before the Lord she sought all her life. It was January 27, 1540 when our Saint who consoled so many during her lifetime, would now have to console her charges from Heaven.

In 1544, four years after her death, Pope Paul III published a Bull officially affirming the Company of St. Ursula was a congregation.

In 1568, there were four depositions from witnesses who had known Angela Merici during her lifetime. Two centuries had to pass before the cause of Beatification was opened. In 1768, it was decreed by Clement XIII that Angela now deserved to bear the title *Blessed.* And in 1807, Pius VII canonized Angela Merici and Saint Angela Merici entered the Royal Communion of Saints. In 1866, Pope Pius IX extended her cult from Italy, to the entire Universal Church.

When Bob, Rob[16] and I first met our Sisters of the Company of Angela Merici in 1977, we were completely fascinated by these women, never realizing at the time how they and their foundress would one day influence our lives, and how we would this day write about this Super Saint for all time, Angela Merici. We went, originally, out of curiosity because we had heard her body was incorrupt, and found a powerful Saint and Role Model for today and all the days to come. *Please pray for us, Saint Angela Merici.*

---

[16]Bob and Penny's grandson at age 10

Saint Dominic - Watchdog of God

"I give you arms, with which throughout your life
you may fight against the devil."

Arming a young man with the double-edge sword of which St. Paul spoke, St. Dominic intoned these words, as he vested him in the habit of the *Friars Preachers*. This would be Dominic's will and testimony, the legacy he would leave, to all the young and courageous who would pick up his torch and lead the way to Jesus.

The birth of a Saint

Our story takes us to Spain, a *Christian* part of Spain recently freed from more than four hundred years of cruel domination. The small, sleepy village of Caleruega, resting unnoticed between the lofty cities of Burgos and Segovia,[1] will bring the world a treasury of Saints. If we travel back in time, we can see turrets and ramparts majestically dominating the horizon, proudly announcing the nobility who dwell within. Today, all that is left of the grandeur of yesterday, is the tower of the Guzmán palace, where a Saint and two Blesseds lived and loved. Our story is about the Saint - Dominic. In 1170, he was born into the nobility of this world;[2] he and his family predestined to be part of that nobility; but *instead* that nobility would produce souls who would spend their life journeying toward *eternal* life with the nobility in Heaven.

Saints beget Saints, as we will see in our story of one of the greatest Defenders of the Faith, Mother Church has ever raised to the Heavenly Halls of Canonized Saints, Saint Dominic - Founder of the Order of Friar Preachers.

Dominic's father was Felix Guzmán, commander of knights, the brave and loyal knights who were instrumental in

---

[1]This area was reconquered in 1040 A.D. The entire country was reconquered after 700 years of domination.
[2]both parents from old Castilian nobility

Above: ***Saint Dominic***
The Watchdog of God

Right: ***Saint Dominic consecrated***
himself and dedicated his life to the
salvation of souls

Above: ***Our Lady and Baby Jesus present the Rosary to St. Dominic***
Entrance to Our Lady of the Rosary Basilica - Lourdes, France

recovering Spain for Christ. During the stormy, bloody days of her resurrection from slavery, he and his army protected the borders of Christian Spain, defending her against the fierce and determined hordes of Moors[3] advancing on Castille, where his palace was located.

Dominic's mother Juana of Aza was also of an old Castilian family, of the nobility like her husband. But this mother because of the life she led and the great influence she had on her children would be declared Blessed. She would raise a future Saint - Dominic, and a Blessed - her oldest son Mannes; historians conjecture they wouldn't be surprised if her other son Anthony would also be raised to a Blessed, as he died caring for victims of the plague.

Before Dominic was born, his mother Juana had a prophetic vision of a dog carrying a lit torch in his mouth, igniting everything in his path, as he sped throughout the world. She was confused and troubled by the vision and went to pray at the Shrine of St. Dominic of Silos,[4] after whom she later named her third son, Dominic. [This is how we often see images of St. Dominic - accompanied by a dog with a lit torch in his mouth.]

There was another prophecy foretelling the destiny of this special child. When his godparents held the baby Dominic over the font to be baptized, his godmother saw a brilliant star shining on his forehead. When later writing of St. Dominic, authors and historians often recount these two incidents, the one with the dog and the one with the star. Almost everyone who knew him testified that a *certain splendor* always radiated from his face, as if from a star.

God, with His Eyes on those He has chosen, placed our future Saint into a home filled with virtue and piety, his mother praying with her children, bringing them closer to God and His Will for them. It will not come as a shock, therefore, when her

---

[3]Moslem
[4]Dominic of Silos was a Holy Benedictine abbot, after whom the Shrine was named.

child Dominic chooses the path to holiness and sainthood. The only problem is that before Dominic was born, his two older brothers were already preparing for the priesthood. The estate and the father's responsibilities passed to the only son left, Dominic!

[With many Latin families, Mama rules, with the key she holds to their hearts. Juana was declared Blessed for the part she played in bringing about the miracle that came to pass in this noble house. Destined to produce brave knights for Spain, instead the House of Guzmán brought forth loyal knights to serve God in His royal Priesthood.]

What did Juana do? Knowing in her heart that this child, too, belonged to God, she sent Dominic at age seven, to her brother, who just happened to be a priest! Dominic studied under his uncle, learned how to serve as an altar boy, was made proficient in Latin and learned the tenets of our Faith. That might have been where it ended and Dominic would have grown into a very holy knight, in the world. But again God, the Master Chess-Player, has set His pieces in place strategically! Gumiel d'Izan, where Dominic was staying, was on the way to Santiago de Compostela. Pilgrims, on the way to the Shrine, to plead with Santiago (St. James) to intercede with God for deliverance from the Moors, always stopped in Gumiel d'Izan to rest. They recounted the torture and atrocities inflicted on those who dared practice their Catholic Faith, adding they were *personally* exposed to the Moors' *"conquer through terror"* technique that was being carried out even in Christian Spain.

We never know what our children are taking to heart; was this when the seed was planted in Dominic's heart to go and preach to the millions of pagans who did not know Jesus and the Church He founded? At age fourteen, Dominic left for Palencia to broaden his studies. We know little of those days, except it has been told that when Dominic encountered refugees who were starving and had no shelter, he sold all his books and gave them the money. Now, possibly today that might not mean much, but in those days, before the printing press, all books were copied by hand; so Dominic had no books to study and little or no opportunity to have them replaced. But when questioned he replied, *"How can I study from dead skins when living men are starving?"*

As his Lord before him, Dominic had an urgency about him - too much to do with too little time to do it. This and his thirst for knowledge, he would pass on to future preachers who would follow. He was charismatic and filled with compassion for those starving not only from lack of food but the Word of God. This passion for God and His children would draw many young men and women to him in the days ahead. His life, filled with days and nights of peaceful but exciting pursuits of holiness, was to come to full fruition, the day Dominic was ordained to the priesthood in around 1195.

Now 25 years old, Dominic realized his walk was not as a secular priest but as a religious. At that time, Dominic's bishop Martin Bazan voiced a desire to bring about reform; he wanted the canons of his cathedral to live a shared life as *religious*, as part of a community. He and the new prior of the canons, Don Diego de Asevedo, had heard of Dominic's piety and wisdom, and his desire to be a religious. Their hope was that he could convince these self-absorbed, strong-willed clerics into coming together and join the Canons Regular; they summoned Dominic! So after he was ordained a priest, Dominic was vested in the habit of the Canons Regular of Osma, made his profession to that Order, and for the next nine years faithfully followed the Rule of St. Augustine. One of his companions said of him, at this time,

"Now it was that he began to appear among his brethren like a bright burning torch, the first in holiness, the last[5] in humility, spreading about him an odor of life which gave life, and a perfume like the sweetness of summer days. Day and night he was in the church praying without ceasing. God gave

---

[5]meaning he is always last to receive or taking the last place

him the Grace to weep for sinners and for the afflicted; he bore their sorrows in an inner sanctuary of compassion which pressed on his heart, flowed out and escaped in tears. It was his custom to spend his nights in prayer and to speak to God behind closed doors. "[6]

Dominic consecrated himself, dedicating his life to the salvation of souls for Christ. He was happy! He thought this was where God had placed him, but that was to come to an end, when Don Diego, now Bishop of Osma, chose him to accompany him on a mission to Denmark, which would be the first leg of a long journey of suffering, pain and torment.

As they traveled through southern France, Dominic's heart felt like it would bleed to death, as he encountered the enormous suffering brought about by a new threat against the Church and her children - the Albigensian Heresy. The churches were empty; the bells no longer tolled; Sunday you could see people working in the fields. There was a funereal spirit over the villages, as if God Himself was moaning over the death of His children's souls. They were like men, women and children walking in their sleep through a dark cloud shutting out all sun.

Tired and downcast, Dominic and the bishop stopped at an inn in Toulouse, only to discover that the innkeeper was a heretic. Dominic could not go peacefully to sleep, while there was the danger that a soul could be lost. He talked to the man throughout the night, showing him the error of this heresy and the long-range effects disobedience has first on one soul and then on those he encounters. Dominic, clarifying the errors put forth by the heretics, and bringing him the true teachings of the Faith, when dawn came peeking into the dark of night, the innkeeper's heart and soul were filled with the same light which flooded the room; he renounced the heresy and pledged to follow the true teachings of Mother Church.

---

[6]p.6 Saint Dominic by Sister Mary Jane Dorcy. O.P. - TAN Publications

Was it here that the seed to start a religious Order, dedicated to defending the Church, correcting errors and bringing the Truth to the faithful, was planted in Dominic's heart?

Dominic turns to Our Lady for help

Dominic always turned to his Heavenly Mother for help! When Dominic and the bishop visited the Court of France, they found the Queen grieving deeply because she had no children. Dominic told her to pray the Rosary. Not only did she adopt this prayer, she brought that devotion to all the citizens in her realm, asking them to join her in praying for a male child who would wear the crown of France, one day. A boy was born, the future St. Louis of France. They prayed the Rosary, softened the Heart of God, and a future Saint was born; a great Saint was given to the Church and to the world!

Their mission was successfully completed in Denmark. But God had a greater plan in mind. Seeing the death of faith overtaking the world, before they returned to Spain, the bishop and Dominic stopped in Rome. Bishop Diego asked to be relieved of his bishopric, so that he could spend the rest of his days correcting the heresies that were rotting away the very foundation of the Church. Both he and Dominic had been witnesses, seeing with their own eyes the devastating attacks upon Mother Church from all fronts, with hordes of heathens laying siege on Christ's Kingdom on Earth[7] on one front, and those within the Church attacking on another, the enemy of God flanking her on all sides with relentless attacks, leaving her, dear Mother that she is, bleeding.

Having seen the helplessness of the faithful in the Nordic countries,[8] the bishop and Dominic asked Pope Innocent III for permission to go to Tartary[9] and the Pope refused! They stopped at the Abbey of Citeaux with the idea of becoming Cistercians, then decided against it, as the bishop realized his first

---

[7] the Catholic Church
[8] on their trip to Denmark
[9] referring at that time to an area including Russia and Manchuria

responsibility was to the diocese that had been entrusted to him. They had hoped to receive the deep scarlet crown of Martyrdom among the heathen in Tartary; that was not to come to pass. They had desired to live among the Cistercians; that was not to be. Eager to serve God and Church but not knowing how it would come to pass, they resignedly turned their eyes toward Spain, believing that God's Will lay in their obedience to the Pope.

Dominic joins the battle to combat the *Albigensian Heresy*

On their way, they stopped at Montpellier. There, they discovered a pot of errors bubbling, spilling over dangerously into every walk of life. No one and nothing was free from the *Albigensian Heresy*[10] which threatened to drown the Church. How were these heretics able to attract so many? First of all, like cults of today, such as the Jehovah Witnesses, they provided for their bodily needs. They gave people easy answers to the many evils in their lives, many of which they brought about themselves. The heretics delivered fiery, very dramatic sermons; in those days, our priests did not deliver *any* sermons. Many of our priests led lives of wealth and comfort, and their parishioners went hungry; whereas, the heretics gave generously to their followers, while leading a very austere lifestyle. Of course, everything they gave came from other followers. Was Jesus going to allow these misguided children of His be lost? No, He sends Saints into the melee to fight the good fight!

During the papacy of Innocent II, Albigensianism was spreading like wildfire throughout southern France. The Pope

---

[10]"This heresy gathered all the heresies of the past and put them into one presentation. Their philosophy or false theology used Paganism as well as Christianity to entice the unsuspecting looking for something new! Those within the Church, who are spreading errors today, are doing the very same thing as the Albigensians before them." From Bob and Penny Lord's book, *"Scandal of the Cross and Its Triumph, Heresies throughout the History of the Church."* You will find this heresy and other heresies that have attacked the Church for the last 2000 years, in this book.

put the job in the hands of the Cistercians. First, he sent two; when they weren't successful, he sent another two. Then he sent in *thirty Cistercians*, twelve of them abbots. These were the most disciplined, most learned religious of the times; but compared to the austerity of the heretics, their lifestyle was relaxed and easygoing. It became obvious that it would take more than these followers of St. Bernard of Clairvaux.

Now a new Pope in power, Innocent III turned to Dominic and the Bishop of Osma for help in erasing this threat from the Church. St. Dominic and the bishop went to the Cistercians and appealed to them to live a more heroic life, a life which more exemplified that of the Savior Whom they were called to imitate. St. Dominic and the bishop told them that the common folk joined the Albigensians *more* because of the life they saw them leading, than by their preaching. They asked the Cistercians to cease traveling by horse with an entourage, to no longer stay at comfortable inns, with servants to wait upon them. Dominic said that first they had to begin by truly living the Gospel, then the people would listen to gentle persuasion and loving dialogue. This, rather than intimidation and dictatorial pressure is what would bring heretics back to the Church. The Cistercians wanted no part of this so they left.

As *Albigensianism* was considered now more a religion than a heresy, it was extremely dangerous to evangelize and preach against it. The Heretics did not want to lose their brainwashed followers, who would do almost anything for their false gods, the Heretics. And so they were not above using force. At the recommendation of Don Diego, the Bishop of Osma, Dominic and his followers were sent into the area to live, much like Francis and his followers were living in central Italy. There were seventy two of them. They carried no money, no staff, no possessions. They truly lived the austere Gospel life, in an effort to convert by example. And against overwhelming odds, convert they did! The example they set bore fruit, and by the end of ten years, there were a great deal of conversions. But Albigensianism was still very strong and firmly entrenched.

Dominic begins to open houses for former heretics

Because so many noble families had lost all they had as a result of the horrible war which had stripped everyone of all their possessions, many of their children had no recourse but to attend schools provided by the Albigensianists. They were actually sold into slavery to the Heretics. Dominic combated this by setting up *convent* schools available to teach the True Faith. The Church was not proficient in the ways of the world, ill-equipped to combat this insidious poison, now being promulgated by some of the most respected families. Dominic knew the only answer was to organize the Church, and engage in a Gentle Revolution!

Where did Dominic go? Now Dominic had always had a deep devotion to the Mother of God. One evening, as he was praying on a hill in Prouille, overlooking the Shrine of *Our Lady of Prouille*, a church he frequented on his journeys through the southern part of France, he saw a globe of fire shoot down from the heavens and come to hover over the little chapel. Dominic took this as a sign from Heaven this was where he was to establish his first convent. The first nine sisters were converts from the Albigensian Heresy; they initially came to Dominic, seeking asylum from their families, who had been thoroughly indoctrinated into the Albigensian Cult. Like his dear friend Francis of Assisi with St. Clare, these nine had not only heard Dominic preach the Truth but most exemplify what he preached; their eyes were opened, and they wanted that Truth Who alone can make them free. They were to be a cloistered community devoted to the education of young women in danger of being exploited by the Albigensianists. At that time he also opened a friary for the brothers who came to serve.

Time came for his good friend and mentor, Bishop Diego to go back to Spain and his diocese. His promise to send reinforcements, to help Dominic, never came to pass, as he died soon after arriving home. With the news of his death, instead of more help, the few Dominic had, returned to Spain. Now, alone, with the monumental task God had given him, Dominic committed himself to the Lord as His *solitary* preacher, if need be. As if that was what God was waiting for, another friend and mentor entered into his life, Foulques, Bishop of Toulouse. Like Dominic, he had a fiery passion to serve Mother Church. This was truly a gift from God, for one of Dominic's greatest crosses was the lack of courage and determination he found among the bishops and clergy, the absence of strength required to act upon and fulfill the Will of God. For the next ten years, this prelate would be Dominic's benefactor, affirming him when he was in most need, the right arm Dominic needed in the face of endless adversity.

It was time! Dominic began the Order of Preachers, better known today as the Dominicans.[11] He founded a house for Albigensianists who wished to leave the sect. Everything was going fine, until the local Count of Toulouse tried to close the house down. The Count had allowed the heretics to operate freely, to serve his own political ends. The sect controlled a considerable voting block, and was very influential. St. Dominic was causing problems for the Count; he couldn't allow him to continue.

A papal legate is assassinated, and war breaks out!

Pope Innocent III sent his papal legate Peter of Castelnau, to resolve the matter quickly. Peter tried to dissuade the Count from supporting the heretics, to no avail. As the Count would not cease his attack on the Church, Peter had no recourse but to excommunicate him. In addition, the Count, Raymond of Toulouse had broken every promise made to the Church. When the excommunication was announced, the Count sent two of his henchmen, who waylaid and killed the legate of Rome.

Peter of Castelnau had spent his life preaching on the Word Who is God. Dying, he would end his life just as the

---

[11]Dominicans or *Domine Cane* which means God's Watchdogs.

Word before him, his last words, asking forgiveness for his murderers. Turning to the missionaries he was leaving behind, Peter told them to be strong and carry on this most solemn work of saving the lost lambs of the Church.

Peter of Castelnau was bitterly hated by the heretics. He often said: *"Religion will not raise its head in Languedoc until it is watered by the blood of a martyr."* As he lay there, he fulfilled his own prophecy, the ground soaked by his blood, he was martyred for the Faith. Never compromising, this legate, named after our first Pope, died as he had lived, faithful to the Church, to the end!

When news of Peter of Castelnau's death reached Pope Innocent III, he sent letters to the kings of France and Spain to lay aside their differences, their self-interests and unite behind the banner of the Church and fight this *"rage of heresy."*[12] It was no longer a war between ideological differences; words were no longer the sole means of attack; the Church was being raided by armed thieves vandalizing and stripping churches and convents; then leaving nothing - burning them to the ground.

Maligned and defamed, Mother Mary cries for her Dominic

The man placed in charge of the Catholic combined forces, was the legate - Arnold of Citeaux; it was *not Dominic*! Dominic played a very minor role in this campaign, nothing more than that of a *chaplain* serving the crusaders' souls: and yet after the Reformation of the Sixteenth Century the word was that it was Dominic, *"the infamous preacher"* who caused the bloodshed of the Albigensian war. This accusation is so against his most gentle character, his compassionate heart and soul, it makes one weep to hear him so maligned. But as always, from the time of Adam and Eve, when the father of lies called God a liar, the innocent have been attacked by the guilty, the holy by the wicked. It began in the Garden of Eden and witless instruments

---

[12]quoting Pope Leo III - Saint Dominic by Sister Mary Jane Dorcy. O.P. - TAN Publications

of the devil have carried on his work, and will, I am afraid, till the Lord comes again.

What was Dominic doing while this bloody encounter was going on? He and the small band who had remained with him, went around the countryside, barefoot, without roof over their heads, completely dependent on alms, preaching the Word of God; and if that makes him the *"bloody Dominic"* they called him, then please Lord allow us to walk beside such as he.

The mission bestowed upon him and Bishop Diego by Pope Innocent III never having been rescinded, Dominic continued to carry out the role of reconciling heretics to the Church and assigning them penances. For this he was given the name of *"First Inquisitor,"* which could not have been more misleading. There is *no entry* in history of Dominic's participation in the Inquisition! Had he played the crucial role they have discredited him with, there assuredly would be some mention in the annals of that period. Furthermore, as no such office existed before the Lateran Council of 1215, and it was in 1230, nine years after Dominic's death that the Council of Toulouse assigned a share of the governing body to the Friars Preachers, Dominic would have had to have exercised his duty from the grave.

In addition, when the jurisdiction was originally handed down, to judge and, upon finding guilty, denounce heretics, it was not assigned to the Dominicans but to the Cistercians! At that time, Dominic lived in Fanjeux and Carcassonne, more than one hundred miles from Toulouse, near his Lady of Prouille. He preferred to be known simply and humbly as the parish priest of Fanjeux. He would walk seventeen miles each day to Carcassonne to people who scoffed at him, leveled abuses at him, threw dirt and stones at him, all the time calling him foul names, making a sport of playing him for the fool; and he, the great fool of Christ came back for more.

One day, coming upon a gang of heretics, about whom he had been forewarned, he calmly passed through them joyfully singing hymns. Possibly stunned by his bravery, they did not carry out their plan to kill him. But later, having recovered, they confronted him, again, and challenged him, threatening, *"So you're not afraid to die. What would you have done if we began killing you?"* Dominic replied, *"I would beg you to not finish me with one quick blow but little by little."* They avoided him, from that time on, believing being killed was just what he wanted.

Our Lady gives St. Dominic the Rosary

The heresy of Albigensianism, which had started in Southern France in the Eleventh Century, had become a deadly cancer threatening the entire Church. Although he would fight with all his might to defeat this heresy, it was an uphill fight. He prayed for help. The Angels brought his prayer to the feet of Our Lady. One night in 1208, while St. Dominic was hard at prayer in the Chapel of Notre Dame de la Prouille,[13] Our Lady appeared to him. Holding the Rosary, She said,

"Be of good courage, Dominic; the fruits of your labor shall be abundant. The remedy for the evils which you lament will be meditation on the life, death and glory of my Son, uniting thereto the recitation of the Angelic Salutation (Hail Mary) by which the mystery of redemption was announced to the world.

"This devotion you are to inculcate by your preaching, is a practice most dear to my Son and to me - as a most powerful means of dissipating heresy, extinguishing vice, propagating virtue, imploring divine mercy, and obtaining my protection. I desire that not only you, but all those who shall enter your Order, perpetually promote this manner of prayer. The faithful will obtain by it innumerable advantages and will always find me ready to aid them in their wants. This is the precious gift which I leave to you and to your spiritual children."[14]

---

[13]to whom St. Dominic had a great devotion
[14]Taken from Bob and Penny Lord's book, *"The Rosary, the Life of Jesus and Mary"* pgs 182-183

Dominic begins preaching on the Rosary

War and hate killing the innocent, who did not know why they were fighting, or for that matter being killed, it was time for the Mother of God to instruct Her children through Dominic as to the true meaning of the Rosary, Her Life and that of Her Son Jesus. She was calling them to meditate on what Mary and Jesus' 'yes cost Them. Although the Rosary had been prayed for generations before the Blessed Mother came to Dominic, it was more of a vocal repetitious praying of Hail Mary's, Glory be's and Our Father's fingering the beads of the Rosary. With Mother Mary giving him this new mission, he was able to have the whole Church participate with Her and Her Son in what They lived through, that we might be saved.

So, we see Dominic, in the midst of hell, with the rabid dog of war wildly, indiscriminately attacking the innocent along with the guilty, no one exempt; and he is preaching the Rosary! Does this sound incredulous? Do we not need to say the Rosary, today, meditating on how Our Lord and Our Lady walked to the Cross for us, how this Church which has been so under attack for the last 2000 years flowed from the pierced Heart of Jesus? Do we think about the price He paid for the Church? Is this what gave them the courage to climb insurmountable heights and face unbeatable foes? When the Albigensianism heresy was finally defeated, Dominic gave full credit to the intercession of *Our Lady of the Rosary.*

Our Lady of the Rosary intercedes and the war is won!

Dominic became vicar to the Bishop of Carcassonne. But his peace was to be short-lived. Things were out of hand, conditions deplorable. Life would again change for him, along with the course of the Albigensian war. As war is about power more than ideology, more sons would have to die to satisfy man's gluttonous appetite for might. As this was a war over men's souls, neither side would give up, the knowing ordering and the unknowing following, *"Rachel was once more crying for her children."*[15]

Peter, the King of Aragon, marched into Carcassonne with his massive forces and united them with the Albigensian soldiers. The defenders of Mother Church were so overwhelmingly outnumbered, only a miracle would save her. A council was called in Muret to determine what course to take. Dominic was summoned and went hurriedly to Muret; but on the way he stopped to pray before the tomb of St. Vincent the Martyr. When one of the canons sought him out, he beheld Dominic levitated in ecstasy before the altar.

September 10th, the King of Aragon converged on Muret with forty thousand men. The Count of Montfort was caught with only eight hundred men. With no other course possible, the Count advised his forces he was going to abdicate. He went into the chapel to prepare himself for the inevitable, his death. At the suggestion of Dominic, the Catholic forces began praying the *Rosary*. The Count of Montfort, fully clad in his resplendent knight's armor knelt before the bishop and, after receiving his blessing, solemnly pledged his undying love and faithfulness to the God and Church through the Mother of God, *"I consecrate my blood and life for God and His Faith."* The Rosary having been said, the troops marched out to battle and the priests retired to the church to pray.

The Count of Muret and his small army, first charged, then made as if to retreat, and then charged once again, only furiously this time, plowing right through the middle of the thousands of advancing soldiers, clear to the center of the camp, where King Peter of Aragon and his nobles were seated. Completely dazed and dejected by the unexpected coup, his army deserted, leaving the king dead.

And where was Dominic throughout the battle? He was *not*, as some very prejudiced historians like to write (fabricating

---

[15]Mt 2:18

for their own agendas), in front of the attacking forces leading them on to victory. This would have been impossible; he had absolutely no training in the art of war. More accurate and honest is that he was with other priests and the women praying for the brave men whom they believed were going to a certain death.

Innocent III calls the Council of Lateran

Dominic was returning to Rome with Bishop Foulques of Toulouse. It had been eleven years since his first visit with Bishop Diego of Osma. So much had happened! Innocent III was still the Pope and had called the Council of Lateran, which has gone down in history as second only to the Council of Trent in importance to our Faith. Hundreds and hundreds of bishops, abbots and friars, along with heads of all the Royal houses of Europe were there to discuss the condition of the world. This council defined some of the most important tenets of our Faith. From her very inception, Mother Church has called councils to declare dogmas which we have always believed from the very beginning, but have not defined until attacked. Thanks to the Heresy of Albigensianism, the Council defined Church doctrine addressing this and other heresies[16] which threatened to sink the Barque of Peter.[17]

Pope Innocent III recognizes Dominic and his brothers

Ten years before the commencement of the Council of Lateran, there had been a flurry of preachers, often uneducated, tickling the ears of the unknowing faithful with errors. They were, for the most part anti-clerical and anti-papal. So, it was with some apprehension and caution that Innocent, although he knew of Dominic's reputation, opened himself to presenting Dominic's brief to the bishops. As the Church had ruled no new

---

[16]For more heresies that have attacked the Church and been dispelled by Councils, read Bob and Penny Lord's book: *"Scandal of the Cross and Its Triumph"-Heresies throughout the History of the Church.*
[17]Ship of the Church

Orders be founded, the Pope advised Dominic to return home and
choose one of the older Rules. It was at this time that the Pope
had a dream and recognized the two friars holding up St. John
Lateran,[18] as Francis of Assisi and Dominic.

After much prayer, Dominic and the brothers decided they
would follow the Rule of St. Augustine.[19]   But the Order of
Preachers is not a duplication of any other Order; it is unique
with its own charism and apostolate. Though affirmed by other
Popes, we quote Pope Clement IV:

*"Your Order is a fortified city which guards the truth and
welcomes the faithful through its portals. It is the sun shining in
the Temple of God, the cypress on the heights, lifting minds that
regard it, the field of the Lord fragrant with celestial roses."*

Pope Innocent III dies; Dominic has a new friend and Pope

It was with a sad heart and more than a little concern that
the brothers received the news that Pope Innocent III had died.
He had been a good friend and supporter of Dominic and his
friars. Nevertheless, Dominic set out for Rome, and approval of
his new community. He arrived in September, only to find that
the new Pope, Honorius was not in Rome. Considering the
work-load awaiting the new Pope, you would think that Dominic
would go home and come back after the Pope was settled. Not
Dominic! He slept in the churches. Believing in the Son's love
for His Mother, Dominic prayed to his most precious Blessed
Virgin for her intercession.

She came through! In December of that same year, just
three short months after being elevated to the Chair of Peter,
Pope Honorius issued the first Bull granting Dominic certain
privileges and impunities, with rights to formerly held lands,
churches and property which had been donated by Bishop
Foulques of Toulouse. In the second Bull which was much
shorter than the first, Honorius referred to them as *"champions of*

---

[18]the Pope's church as Bishop of Rome
[19]the oldest Rule of the Church

the faith." What an awesome privilege and opportunity, as well as responsibility, this heritage carries for all the men and women religious who make up the Order of Preachers.

Eager to get back to his family of preachers, and be about his mission of evangelizing to those who had left the Church, Dominic would have to wait once more upon the Lord's timetable. Always believing that God speaks through the Pope, Dominic peacefully remained with the Holy Father, who, like his predecessor, had also grown fond of Dominic. He was commissioned to be the Pope's theologian, where he was required to teach before the court and the Cardinals, and appointed as censor[20] of all books, an office filled by a Dominican till today. While there Dominic made another friend, one who would become the future Pope Gregory IX. As Cardinal, he was familiar with the work of the two powerful living Saints the Lord had raised up for this crucial time in the Church, and loved Francis and Dominic.

Finally Dominic was able to return to Toulouse and his community. The whole village turned out! His friars were filled with joy! Their merriment was short-lived when the time came to tell them they must part. Dominic explained that the work was great and the laborers few; they would have to go out, two by twos, to countries near and far, to preach the Good News, strengthening those who had remained in the Catholic Church and bringing back those who had strayed. Everyone advised him against this move, but he insisted saying some of the wisest words I have ever heard:

"Do not oppose me, for I know very well what I am doing. The seed will moulder (decay) *if it is hoarded up; it will fructify* (bear fruit) *if it is sown."*

It was the Feast of the Assumption in 1217, when Dominic chose to announce that this was to be the last time they would all be assembled under one roof. He celebrated the Mass. All the

---

[20]to determine which books were in agreement with the Magisterium and which contained serious errors.

people of Languedoc were there. He preached, as he had never before. He told the parishioners because of their hard hearts, their blindness, he and the apostolate had come to realize that they would have to leave and settle elsewhere. Then he turned to his brothers and told them to always have the courage to speak the truth.

Dominic continued to live a simple life, wearing the same patched, worn tunic in the *freezing* winter and the *suffocating* summer. In the evening, after a hard day's work, he would spend his evening hours praying at the different altars in the church, often found in the morning having fallen asleep on the altar steps. He would do penance, flagellating himself first for his sins, then for those of sinners, and third for the Poor Souls in Purgatory. He would get so involved with the ongoing *Sacrifice of the Cross*, the Sacrifice of the Mass that he would weep throughout the consecration when Jesus comes to us, Body, Blood, Soul and Divinity. He was deeply involved in the formation of those in his care; as a holy father chastising his children when necessary, and then balancing with generous compassion at other times.

Pope Honorius gave them the church of St. Sixtus located on the Appian Way to use for a convent. Miracles began from the very beginning! They were digging beneath the old building when a huge mass of dirt fell smothering a worker beneath the rubble. The friars ran to save him, but saw it was too late! However not for Dominic; he began to pray, as he simultaneously instructed the brothers to dig! Imagine their amazement when having removed all the earth, there was the man alive and breathing.

The Pope and his predecessor Innocent III had been trying to *reform* the women religious in Rome to no avail. This would be the mission assigned to Dominic. It was no mean task; they had gotten used to this casual life and did not want anyone interfering, especially men. They were women of wealthy families who encouraged them to be independent; they had seriously relaxed the rules of cloister life, having visitors at all hours of the day or night; their superiors had little or no authority; they would not even listen to the Cardinals!

Dominic proposed giving up his convent to a group of Nuns, who were living in St. Mary on the Tiber convent. Although it met with fierce opposition initially, the abbess agreed, with the proviso that a miraculous picture of Our Lady come with them; Dominic agreed. All was in order when the Nuns repented of their promise and refused to move. Dominic went to their convent and celebrated Mass for them; as he spoke so compassionately, their hearts were moved, they agreed to move into the convent at St. Sixtus and go into deep cloister.

But Dominic, wise father that he was, took the keys to the convent and made the brothers porters of the door, with strict instructions the Nuns not be allowed to have families and friends visit, except at assigned times. Their piety and joy became well known in Rome and attracted more young women. This became the second convent under St. Dominic.

We would just like to share a miraculous occurrence that Dominicans speak of till today. One day the brothers had been unsuccessfully begging for alms all day and were dejectedly returning to the convent when they met up with a woman. Feeling compassion on them, she gave them a loaf of bread. They walked a few steps when they were stopped by a poor man begging; he asked them for their loaf of bread. They, at first, insisted that it was all they had, but upon his persisting pleading turned the bread over to him. Now, while this was happening, the Lord had enlightened St. Dominic what had come to pass, so when the brothers approached he asked them if they had returned with nothing! When they recounted what had transpired, he said, *"Have no fear; it was an Angel of the Lord."*

Dominic summoned the whole community to come and eat in the refectory. He insisted, over their protests, they prepare the tables for their nightly meal. They were all seated; Dominic gave the blessing and one of the brothers began to read, aloud. Dominic prayed! Suddenly two handsome young men appeared and began distributing bread. After the last loaf was dispensed, they disappeared. Then Dominic instructed the community to eat the bread the Lord had provided. Dominic then charged the brothers to pour the wine; and when they said there was none, he insisted they obey him, take the vessels and pour the wine which the Lord has provided. They obeyed and they not only filled all the glasses, they had enough wine and bread for three days! The third day, Dominic instructed them to keep none, but give the rest to the poor.

The Friar Preachers had worn the habit of the Augustinians when the Mother of God appeared and gave them the habit they wear till today. A new brother was entertaining joining the Order; he had just met Dominic when he fell seriously ill. The young man, Reginald, was on his death bed; Dominic began pleading for the healing of this child whom the Lord had just given him, only to be taken away from him so quickly. Our Lady answered Dominic's plea by appearing to Reginald, the ailing young man, accompanied by two breathtakingly beautiful handmaidens from Heaven. She told him to ask what he willed and she would grant it. Just as he began searching in his heart what to ask for, one of the maidens suggested he leave it up to Our Lady. Our Lady anointed his head, *"his eyes, nostrils, mouth, hands and feet."*[21] As she anointed his feet, She said, *"Let your feet be shod for the preaching of the Gospel of Peace."* Then she showed him the habit the Order was to wear. No one would have known of Our Lady's appearance, if it had not been Her wish the Order know of the habit she had chosen for them to wear. Reginald begged Dominic not to tell the brothers what had happened till after he was dead. Dominic did as he had requested, then gave the Order the habit; but did not disclose the origin till one year later, when Reginald went to dwell with his Fair Lady, his Mother Mary.

---

[21]Saint Dominic by Sister Mary Jane Dorcy. O.P. - TAN Publications

A tradition that has transcended time states that Dominic was a man who went preaching through the cities drawing hearts to him like a magnet. Dominic visited all his communities. He left Rome to visit Bologna and remained a short time; then he was on his way to Spain. Dominic arrived in Segovia! He was so happy; this was his native land; they understood him! But there was a sadness that crippled the people of Segovia; they were starving; a drought had robbed them of their crops. One day, as they were all gathered around, he exclaimed: *"Fear not, my brothers, but trust in God's Divine Mercy. I bring you Good News. Today the Lord will shower rain down from Heaven and the drought will be no more."* It came to pass that very afternoon; the people were drenched before they could arrive home! In Segovia, he formed a *Confraternity of the Holy Rosary*, and is known there as the *Saint of the Preachers of the Rosary.*

Dominic went to Paris, to direct those working in the apostolate, and to draw others to join. Then he was off to Italy and on May 27, 1220 Dominic arrived in Bologna, to attend the first General Chapter, which was called to define the rules of the Order. Dominic proposed a democratic form of government. The friars did not always agree with him; for example they all voted for Dominic as *Master General*, against his will. They addressed the slaughter of brothers by heretics against whom they were preaching.

At night, when Dominic walked through the halls, looking in on the friars, he would sometimes encounter the devil walking as well, trying to distract the brothers when they were praying. He would sometimes take on the form of the Blessed Mother and pretending to be her, tell a brother who was disobeying his superiors, or not studying, that he was holy and the Lord was pleased with him. The devil told Dominic that he liked coming to the convent, but disliked the chapter room because of the good accomplished there.

Many times, Dominic would meet up with Blessed Mother, just walking around the convent, checking in on her *little chicks*, sometimes sprinkling them with holy water as they were sleeping. Mother Mary would most often appear with beautiful young women, accompanying Her. This one night Dominic saw Mary sprinkling water on the friars and making the Sign of the Cross on each: but then he noticed she did not bless one of the friars. When he asked her why, she said that the friar wasn't in a state of grace.

Dominic went off to pray and suddenly he went into ecstasy and had a vision of Jesus with the Blessed Mother standing on His right; looking around he saw every Order but his standing before the throne of God. He began to weep, as if his heart would break; the Lord asked him why he wept; to which Dominic replied, *"I weep because I see every Order before You but mine."* The Lord said that that was because He had entrusted his Order to His Mother. Then when the Lord asked him if he desired to see his Order, Mother Mary opened her mantle wide so that it covered all the heavens and underneath were friars extending beyond where the eye could see. With that he awakened from his ecstasy; he called the friars to prayer and began instructing them on the love and veneration owed to the Mother of God, Mary most holy.

It is time for Dominic to go Home

The friars saw Dominic shaky from the fevers that had attacked his already weakened body. They knew the end was near, but they refused to accept it. But Dominic had been foretold by a voice from Heaven that his journey on earth was coming to an end; and that he would serve the Church in Heaven. This did not deter the work he had to do; he spent every drop of energy in his body. But when he returned to Bologna, the friars were alarmed; he had aged so rapidly in the two months he had been on the road. They begged him to go to bed. He insisted on praying the Office with the friars, but could barely stand after the matins[22] were over. His head was swimming.

They tried to put him to bed, but he insisted on being laid on the ground. Then they knew, their father was going Home! He had the friars summoned. His joy belied the drawn lifeless look of death on his face. The brothers tried to keep from crying but failed miserably. The tears streamed down their cheeks; their beloved father was leaving them for the last time. They carried him to a hilltop (thinking the air would help him). He called them to draw near and gave them his last will and testament:

"Have charity toward one another; Guard humility; Make your treasure out of voluntary poverty. You know to serve God is to reign; but you must serve Him in love and with a whole heart. It is only by a holy life and by fidelity to your rule that you can do honor to your profession."

They carried Dominic back to the convent. He was losing ground; one of the brothers wiped the sweat that was pouring down his face. A brother cried out; *"Dear Father, you leave us desolate and afflicted; remember us, and pray for us to God."*

Then Dominic, summoning his last ounce of strength, lifted his eyes and hands to Heaven and prayed:

"Holy Father, since by Thy mercy I have ever fulfilled Thy will, and have kept and preserved those whom Thou hast given me; now I recommend them to Thee. Do keep them; do Thou preserve them."

Then he turned to his children: *"I shall be more useful to you where I am going, than I have ever been in this life."*

He confessed some small sin he thought he had committed and then, arms outstretched to Heaven, he breathed his last breath for Church and community. It was 6 P.M. the 6th of August, 1221. Friars in different parts of Italy and the world reported having seen visions of Dominic rising to Heaven at the time he died.

---

[22]the first and chief hour of the Divine Office

As the church, where St. Dominic's body was entombed, had need of repair, St. Dominic's remains had to wait to be translated. When the church was in readiness, the Cardinal who had been Dominic's friend was now Pope Gregory IX and he gladly gave permission. May 24, 1223, hundreds of friars, with all the Fathers of the Order, bishops, prelates and men of every rank were there solemnly awaiting the translation and subsequent opening of the coffin.

As the dirt parted, and the cement fell away from the tomb, a deep sweet fragrance began to emanate from the sarcophagus; the perfume filled the church when Dominic's coffin was carried in. Tears began to flow from the loving bystanders, as the lid was lifted to reveal their Father just as he had looked two years before when he died. When John of Vicenza, a friar dear to Dominic made way for the bishop, Dominic's body turned to face John; and when John moved again, the body turned once again to face him. With this sign Dominic was saying that he treasured his friars and their love above all honors that could be bestowed upon him.

Miracles upon miracles were reported and verified, far more than was required. It gave Pope Gregory IX the deepest joy to issue a Bull raising Francis, founder of the Friars Minor and Dominic, founder of the Friars Preachers, to the altars of the Church during his pontificate - On July 16th, 1228, Francis was canonized and on July, 1234, Pope Gregory IX declared Dominic a Saint!

Through all the battles, victories and defeats, the Lord used St. Dominic and his followers to save the southern part of Europe from the spreading Albigensianist heresy. The tide turned in 1229 when the University of Toulouse was opened, and the Dominicans became the major teaching influence in the University. It was also at that time, that the Council of Toulouse instituted an Inquisition, unlike the one in Spain, some three hundred years later, which, due to the State's interference with the Church, became more political than religious. The

Dominicans were put in charge, a post they handled with the real spirit of Christianity that their Father and Founder St. Dominic had projected when alive. The Order of Preachers grew and grew, so that in less than a hundred years, they had close to 400 convents in the area that had been infested by the heretics.

The Albigensian heresy was finally put down. If we were to pick one shining light responsible for the ultimate demise of the Albigensian heresy, it would have to be St. Dominic. Our Lord knew who to put in the right place, at the right time, to keep His promise that the forces of hell would not prevail against His Church. Once Dominic and his friar preachers showed that they truly lived what they preached, the heretics were open to hearing the truth: *The Church does not depend on man and his way of life, but on the infallible Word of God, entrusted to the Church by Jesus Himself.* Through their witness they were able to knock down the massive walls blocking the faithful from the Truth, the whole Truth Who dwells in the One, Holy and Apostolic Roman Catholic Church.

God chose a man and filled him with *urgency*, and Dominic used that urgency to found an Order, which would live on after him. For five years after he saw his dream complete, he died, passing on the torch to others.

Right:
St. Elizabeth Ann Seton
She took the vows of
Poverty, Chastity and
Obedience.
She is Foundress of the
Sisters of Charity of St.
Vincent de Paul

Above: **The White House**
The Second home of St. Elizabeth Seton's
Community in Emmitsburg, Maryland

Right: **The Original Chapel in the White**
House of the Second home of
St. Elizabeth Seton's Community in
Emmitsburg, Maryland

St. Elizabeth Ann Seton

"He is more within us than we are ourselves."

St. Elizabeth Ann Seton, or as we knew her when we were children, Mother Seton, is the first American-born Saint we have written about. She was born in New York City, just as we were. When I was a child, I attended a Catholic parochial school, St. Athanasius in the Bronx, taught by those beautiful Sisters of Charity. They wore funny little bonnets which covered their heads, like the pictures you see of Mother Seton, not the type we typically identified with Nuns, especially after having seen Ingrid Bergman in "The Bells of St. Mary." These good Sisters of Charity would read to us from the Lives of the Saints two or three times a week as I recall. These were exciting stories of holy people who had lived good lives, set an example for the world, and went to Heaven. Usually, there were Miracles attached to their lives, or apparitions of Our Lord Jesus and His Mother Mary.

In 1975, we taught CCD to second-graders. Every time we met, we would tell them the story of a Saint whose Feast Day fell on that week. We called them **"Super Saints."** We'd make the Superman insignia on the blackboard, only we'd make two S's for Super Saint. Being as how they were little people, we didn't think they heard a word we told them. But then at Parent-Teacher meetings, when the parents told us how their children came home and told them about this Saint or that one, we knew the Lord had gotten the message across to them. We believe the moving force behind this book and television series came from the stories we heard from these beautiful Sisters of Charity.

These sisters would also tell us stories about their Foundress, Mother Seton, who was not yet a Saint. But she was a very special lady who did great things against tremendous odds, and that's usually the stuff that Saints are made of. So we prayed with the sisters that she would someday become a Saint. The Cause for her Canonization had not been opened at that time, but we didn't know anything about those things. She was a holy lady, and would definitely become a Saint. So all through elementary school, we prayed with the sisters for the Canonization of Mother Seton. But at thirteen, I graduated from that elementary school, went on to High School, and she and her nuns went completely out of my mind. The next time I remember hearing anything about Mother Seton, I had just turned forty years old and five days later on the following Sunday she was canonized a Saint, the first American-born citizen to be raised to the Communion of Saints.

Elizabeth Ann Seton really fits the description of a woman for all seasons. She is truly a role model for women of today. Although she was always a very refined lady, she never shrunk from any kind of work which would help her or her family, whether it be her children or her ladies. She was a personification of motherhood all her life. She was a Protestant who converted after the death of her husband. She was a widow, a single mother, raising five children under the most impossible circumstances in a male-oriented world; she became a nun, and founded a religious community; you name it, Elizabeth Seton did it. Perhaps because she was such a beautiful girl, and was raised in New York society of the period, it seemed to many that she was able to just breeze through life doing wonderful things for the people of God, for the Church and for her family, without raising a bead of perspiration. Her life was anything but that.

However, we are getting ahead of herself. Because the life of Elizabeth Seton covers such a broad spectrum, we wonder sometimes where to begin. There are so many aspects we want to cover, so many important things to tell you, we want to be sure not to leave anything out. But a good rule of thumb is always to begin at the beginning, and let the Lord lead you to where He wants you to go. When He's finished instructing, it's time to end the chapter.[1]

---

[1] *cf* Mother Angelica, when talking about writing her mini-books

Allow me to introduce you to the girl, woman, mother, teacher, Foundress, Saint for whom my precious Grammar School teachers, the Sisters of Charity were praying all those years when I was young, and for the rest of their lives, no doubt. Come and join a woman on her *Journey to Sainthood*, Elizabeth Ann Seton.

New York City was abuzz with activity in 1774. It was two years before we, the people, would declare our Independence from Britain. So while it was exciting in retrospect, it was also covered by a heavy cloud of apprehension. The Boston Tea Party, staged the year before, which brought home the fact that the people of this new world were not happy being taxed up to their hip-boots, without representation. This had not received any positive reaction from the British. But it did send a strong message across the sea that there was unrest and dissatisfaction in the colonies from the people who were supplying a great deal of income to the mother country. New York was a major port and center for immigrants who come from all over the world. A great deal of income was funneling through this town. However, everyone in New York was walking very gingerly, not knowing what next week or next month would bring from the British.

All this tension seemed like a very dim far-off sound to the Bayley family on August 28, 1774, as a newborn baby's cry filled the air. It was the Feast of St. Augustine, but they probably didn't realize it, not being Catholic. However, the Lord knew it, and St. Augustine knew it. So as a special gift to this bold convert, whose mother prayed all those years for his conversion, Our Lord gave St. Augustine on his Feast day, the gift of Elizabeth Ann Bayley.

Nothing is by coincidence. In God's dimension, coincidence does not exist, unless it's Holy Coincidence. So in order to be fully understood, this miracle of our Saint being born on the feast of another powerful Saint, convert, founder of a religious community, Doctor of the Church, the miracle has to be examined in the light of the background from which she came.

Elizabeth Ann Bayley was from a prominent New York family. They had been part of British aristocracy in the old country, and were making quite a name for themselves in this, the new England. Her father, Richard Bayley, was supposed to be an Episcopalian, but he seemed to embrace a fashionable heresy of the time called Deism, popular because it did not really lend its support to any religion. *"Deism accepts the presence of a sort of god who exists and created the world and established certain laws of nature. But Deists maintain that God is not involved in our day-to-day pilgrimage of life, and reject any kind of formal religion or religious practices."*[2] Now I must say that to my way of thinking, Deism is just a term for people who don't believe in religion at all, but want to be Social Christians. For Richard Bayley, Elizabeth's father, religion did not play a part in his life. She recalled that she never heard him mention the name of God in his lifetime, except for once, on his deathbed. That was Elizabeth's religious background on her father's side.

Her mother, Catherine Charlton, was a true Episcopalian, the daughter of an Episcopalian minister, Reverend Richard Charlton, pastor of St. Andrew's Church in Staten Island, New York. We have to believe that Elizabeth received her knowledge of Christianity from this grandfather. She must also have been touched by his great zeal for the people, especially the blacks who were living in poverty in New York City at that time. Of a total population of approximately 30,000 people in 1774, 5,000 were black. So there was a large flock for Pastor Charlton to minister to.

We're not sure how close the Bayleys were to the Charltons. Richard Bayley, a successful doctor and surgeon, was in partnership with Catherine's brother Dr. John Charlton, but

---

[2]*Treasures of the Church, that which makes us Catholic* - Bob and Penny Lord 1997 - Page 69

while Richard and Catherine both lived in Staten Island when they were married, they chose to be married in New Jersey by a different Episcopal minister, rather than at the church where Catherine's father was pastor. It is also believed that Elizabeth was not baptized by her grandfather or at his church. He kept meticulous records, and there is no record in his church of Elizabeth having been baptized there. There is the suggestion of some ill feelings between the two families. It's never explained why that might have been or how it came about.

Richard was in love with his career. Medicine was the other woman in his life. He thought nothing of leaving his family for two years at a time to go off to England to study medicine. The period of time which he chose to do this was not the best either. Relations between the colonies and the British seemed to break down more and more with each passing year. He had gone to England before Elizabeth was born, actually in 1769, the year he and Catherine were married. Their first child, Mary Magdalen, was born while he was in England. She was over a year old when he returned. Then he left them soon after Elizabeth was born, again to England to study.

Now it was 1775. Remember, Elizabeth was born in 1774, when the threat of war was fast becoming a reality. He was not gone a few weeks to England when war broke out between the colonies and England. The Revolutionary War had begun. When Richard finally found his way home on July 12, 1776, he was wearing a British uniform as a surgeon. Now without taking Richard's side, he *was* British. He was born in Connecticut, but his loyalties were with the British. Well, actually, everyone who had any social standing was loyal to the British. Most of the revolutionaries were common folk, like you and me.

But the bulk of the people in what was then the thirteen colonies, knew only one government, that of Grand Brittania. There was no United States; there was not even a Revolutionary government in effect, in 1776. We had just declared our independence from England on July 4th, eight days before Richard came home. The way the whole thing was resolved after the Revolutionary War was over and the United States of America was formed, seemed to be; if you will be patriotic to the new country, and vow allegiance to it, you are an American citizen and all is forgiven. This might be an oversimplification, but basically that was it. We had to get on with the task of building a country. There was no time for vendettas or revenge. We needed all the talent we could muster. Richard Bayley was a good surgeon. The United States needed him. He needed this country. That was it.

Elizabeth's mother, Catherine, was a casualty, not so much of the war, but maybe that was part of it. Perhaps she died because she did not feel loved. Her husband never showed any signs of caring for her or his family. Well, he did love them in his fashion, but they were way down the list of priorities in his life. However, when she was pregnant with their third child, which eventually was the cause of her death, he did try to get leave to come home, and finally gave up his commission with the Military in order to return home. He got there just in time to see the birth of the daughter and the death of the wife. She died on May 8, 1777. Elizabeth had been without a father all her life; now she was without a mother as well. This third child, Catherine, whose birth was the cause of mother Catherine's death, died two years later. Also sadly, her grandfather on her mother's side, Pastor Richard Charlton, died less than six months after his daughter, Catherine. Elizabeth and her sister Mary Magdalen had no one except a father they hardly knew.

Things did not get better for Elizabeth Ann Bayley. Her father married a girl almost half his age, who was in high society. She was the daughter of the family who began the Roosevelt clan in New York. The girl, Charlotte Barclay, never took to Elizabeth or her sister. She took care of them as was required, but never loved them. Elizabeth, for her part, never had a loving word to say about this step-parent. To compound the injury to the children, the second wife Charlotte gave more love and attention to the seven children she sired with Richard Bayley than the two she was stuck with at marriage.

The father also showed no great love for these two daughters when they were young. We can't figure out what Elizabeth and her sister did to the old man to make him treat them so poorly. Were they living signs of how shabbily he had treated his first wife? Was he the cause, to a degree, by his abandonment and lack of caring, of Catherine Charlton Bayley's premature death? It's all speculation, except that when Richard Bayley died, he left everything he had to people other than these two children. The bulk of his estate went to his wife Charlotte and her brood. Another valuable piece of property was left to his mother, who did not need it in the least. So these two dear children, who were born into the cream of society, did not reap the benefits of the *good life*.

To give the father and step-mother some credit, the children did not live a Cinderella's life. They were given all that was necessary to raise them in a manner which would not scream out *scandal* to New York society. But the scandal was there nevertheless, and should have been screamed out. They were never given love. They deserved love, but never got it. That was more a slap in the face than if they had been treated like Cinderellas. They were sent to the best schools, and required to study subjects which would make them acceptable in high society atmosphere, such as the study of French and music. Elizabeth did not care for that much, but in later years, was grateful she had studied these subjects. So in that sense the Bayleys treated them adequately.

Charlotte also taught the children a sense of God. Elizabeth gives Charlotte credit for having taught her how to pray, and how to conceive God. This was possibly the greatest gift she was given in her childhood, one which she would hold onto and not let go. She found God in all this misery, and she could count on that God as a stabilizing force in her life. He was

there always; He never left her. He taught her. He loved her.
He didn't change like the wind, as so many others in her life had.
She wrote of her thoughts of God many years later, *"Every little
leaf and flower, or animal, insect, shades of clouds, or waving
trees, were objects of vacant unconnected thoughts of God and
Heaven."*[3]

Mary and Elizabeth were shipped off to their uncle's estate
in New Rochelle, in Westchester county. He was Richard's
brother, who had semi-retired to that area upstate. He was very
loving to the girls. He was completely different from his brother
in personality. His family loved Mary and Elizabeth as did many
cousins, aunts and uncles, all of whom lived in that area. To be
honest, it was a better life for the girls than in New York City
with their father and step-family. *But they were left there for
four years!* The question that has to shout out to any Christian is
why? What did they do so terrible?

Mary and Elizabeth returned to New York in 1786, for
whatever reason, guilt, or perhaps Charlotte needed help with the
little ones, and thought these two older ones could relieve her of
her burden. They stayed for about two years, until April 1788,
when a major scandal erupted about doctors in the hospital, using
bodies which had been robbed from their graves, as experiments
for medical studies. It took on a ghoulish tone, as New Yorkers
believed their loved ones were being uprooted from their graves
for these fiendish experiments. Riots broke out in the streets,
with people trying to find doctors to punish for what they
believed was an atrocity. It grew to fever pitch, with police
shooting at the mobs and killing some.

Brave Richard Bayley, who may have been responsible for
some of what was going on, took this as a sign to go to England
to study some more. He did to Charlotte what he had done to her
predecessor on more than one occasion. He left her and the
children of both marriages on their own while he fled to England

[3]Mrs. Seton - Joseph Dirvin Pg 16

for a year. He never contacted any of them for that entire time. He had no idea how his family was faring during his absence, and they didn't know if he was alive or dead. Things could not have been going too well for Mary and Elizabeth with Charlotte, their step-mother, because this would have been a perfect time for them to bond, as well as for the girls to help her with her seven children. But the two stepchildren were shipped back to New Rochelle again.

Elizabeth was fourteen years old by this time. She had been used like an emotional yo-yo for most of her life. Her natural adolescent emotions were kicking in and she went through periods of the highest highs and the lowest lows. Although the family in New Rochelle tried to be supportive, they were not her mother or father; they were aunts and uncles. She was sure her father couldn't care less about her well-being. She may have been right! She also didn't know if he was alive. She looked at every cloud to see if her mother or her little sister Kitty (Catherine) might be there to talk to her. She had no one...except God.

Again, a paradox in the life of this powerful Catholic Saint is that her connection with God during her childhood and early teen years was through a Huguenot[4] aunt who taught her all about Christianity. The only problem is that the aunt could not possibly have taught the child objectively, as the Huguenots were the most passionate Anti-Catholic Protestants in Europe. So while Elizabeth never had any desire to join the Catholic Church as a young girl, part of the great miracle is that she didn't hate the Catholic Church and everything to do with it. If we were to recap, a young society girl of New York City, born Protestant but raised without any religious affiliation, abandoned by her father, embraced by a Huguenot aunt, would eventually convert to

---

[4]The followers of Calvin in France were nicknamed Huguenots. The Huguenots suppressed Catholics wherever they could muster power. They hated Catholics more than any Protestant denomination.

Left:
St. Elizabeth Ann Seton
**Fr. Dubourg told her to
keep repeating the
Scripture passage,**
*"The barren woman shall be
the joyful mother of
children."*

Above: ***National Shrine of St. Elizabeth Ann Seton, Emmitsburg, MD***

Catholicism and be the Foundress of a religious community in this country, sounds very far-fetched, if not downright impossible. But with God, nothing is impossible.

We don't want to dwell on her struggles as a young girl. But you must know about them so that you can realize the great miracle which was performed by Our Lord to transform this girl, who should have grown up a very bitter, unhappy adult, into the mother, not only of her own children, but of the many daughters the Lord would send her to parent in her ministry. Through this miracle of the Lord, Elizabeth grew beyond those early years to fulfill her destiny.

Her exile from home and family continued in 1791. The year before, her sister Mary Magdalen had married. For her, the years of unhappiness of not belonging had come to an end. She was five years older than Elizabeth, so one might say she had paid her dues. It was time for a little happiness in her life. It came in the form of Dr. Wright Post, who had been one of Richard Bayley's medical students. While Elizabeth was happy for her sister, she was now alone. She could not stay in New Rochelle. She had always felt she did not belong there, although they had treated her as one of the family. But they were not her family. Her family was in New York City. But when she returned there, it was obvious in a short period of time that she was not welcome there, and so she spent the next four years traveling between her sister's house in New York City and an aunt on her mother's side in Staten Island.

Her time was to come through a prince charming made in Heaven, *William Magee Seton.* They had probably known each other all their lives, but the six years difference in their ages put them in separate worlds. It wasn't until Elizabeth blossomed into a breathtakingly beautiful sixteen year old that William was knocked off his proverbial feet.

This is not unusual. Boys and girls of that age difference can be friends for years until the girl develops into a young lady. First the young boy cannot believe this is the same girl he knew all those years. Then he can't believe he didn't latch onto her years ago. Then he grabs her before it's too late. For her part, the girl cannot understand how this miraculous transformation has taken place in this young man whom she may have secretly loved for years, and she doesn't care. She thanks God and goes with it.

They courted happily through the next few years, living that honeymoon relationship where they could not bear to be separated from each other. The way young people of our time are on the phone with each other so much, young people of their time constantly sent each other notes, even if they were going to see each other the same day. Their romance culminated in a storybook wedding on January 25, 1794, when they were married in sister Mary and brother-in-law Wright's home. The groom was twenty five years old. Elizabeth was nineteen. The world was their oyster.

They lived four glorious years. They were the toast of the town. President Washington had taken up residence in the City, and there were balls and parties galore. And being part of the city's nobility, so to speak, they were part of all that happened. They bought their first house on Wall Street, just a few doors down from the Alexander Hamiltons. They had it decorated just they way they wanted it, and began to build a family. Childbearing was not easy for Elizabeth. She had three children and was pregnant with the fourth when tragedy struck.

Will's father died, leaving seven children to be taken care of plus a business that was having difficulties. Will was the oldest, and was given that responsibility. Poor Elizabeth at her young age, was struggling with her fourth pregnancy and her husband's downcast spirits. They had to give up their house on Wall Street, which just about killed Elizabeth. It was the only house in her twenty-four years which she could call her own. Now they had to move into Will Sr.'s house, because it could accommodate the larger family. She also had to take on a role in the failing business. Between the stress of her family situation and that of the business, she and her baby almost died in the childbirth of her fourth child. Ironically, it was her father, Dr. Richard Bayley, who saved mother and child. He actually breathed life into the child. Possibly, in repayment for this, they named the child after him, Richard Bayley Seton.

That summer, it was as if all the powers of hell raged against Elizabeth Seton and her family. First one child became ill. Then her little one, Richard had problems. They moved out of New York City to what would be considered today uptown, around Seventy-seventh street. In the City, Yellow Fever had broken out and became a great plague. Elizabeth's father spent most of his time working with the stricken. Elizabeth was having trouble with her eyesight, in addition to boils on her body. Will commuted back and forth until he came down with a slight case of Yellow Fever, at which time he had to stay in the family home uptown. He was able to overcome it, but he had to stay away from the downtown section of New York until that dreaded summer of 1798 was over.

But the fall and winter of that year were even worse, not due to physical illness but the rapid decline of the business which Will's father had left in his hands. Will fell into a tremendous depression. He felt the entire burden of taking care of the business and his seven brothers and sisters rested on his shoulders. His father had been a dynamic businessman, well respected and shrewd, but honest. This young man had the honesty, but not the business acumen of the father, nor his standing in the worldwide business community. People tended to take advantage of him because he was vulnerable.

By the end of December, 1800 the business was finished. Will Seton filed for bankruptcy, making a private vow to pay every last penny to his debtors. In those days, the bankruptcy laws were different from today. If a man owed creditors and did not file for bankruptcy, he could be put into debtor's prison. If he did file, he did not have to pay anything other than what he possessed. So Elizabeth, trying to save her husband the final humiliation of listing all their possessions, even to the pairs of socks and underwear which they owned, went through the list with the representative from the Bankruptcy court. Although they were prepared for the worst, they were allowed to stay in their home for another six months. But it was just forestalling the inevitable. They had lost their social standing in New York society. They had lost their beautiful home on Wall Street. His business which had been owned by his father, and which had supported so many of the family, was gone. For William Seton, it was a total disaster.

But it was not really for Elizabeth Seton. This may have been the time which brought her closer to the Lord, and actually headed her in the direction she was to inevitably take. It was as if the Lord was stripping her of everything so that He could remove the scales from her eyes and she could see clearly where she was going and what she was to do. There's an expression, *"When there doesn't seem to be any other option, the Lord must be pointing you in the right direction."* There is a lot of truth in that. We recall some years ago having gone into Louisiana and Texas to give talks at Church Missions. This was right after most of the people had suffered tremendous financial losses, the oil industry having shut down in those states. We recall hearing people on line, waiting for us to sign books, talking to each other.

"I didn't think I was going to make it tonight. I ran out of gas, and I don't have enough money to fill up the tank. But I had to be here."

"I just lost my job today on the oil rigs. Praise God, I feel free."

"I thought I was going to lose my marriage when we were in that country club. Thank God He took all that away from us. We're free in the Lord."

It was hard to understand what those people were saying, how they could be happy in the midst of tragedy. But we hadn't walked in their shoes. We didn't know they were on the brink of despair with all the possessions money could buy. We didn't realize how they were losing their souls through the country clubs and the flirtations with the tennis pro or the lifeguards or the girls at the restaurant or cocktail lounge at the 18th hole, the permissiveness and wife-swapping, drugs and alcoholism and on and on. The Lord had given them the gift of stripping them of their excesses, and freed them of their dependence on things and people. He focused them on the treasures that had true value. *"Where your treasure is, that's where your heart lies."*[5]

We see in the biography of Elizabeth Bayley Seton how her thoughts went from the *frivolous* to the *spiritual*. God had always been an equation in her life, but He was very vague to her. In a happier time, when she had first moved into the house on Wall Street, she wrote: *"My own home at 20 - the world - that and heaven too - quite impossible. My God, if I enjoy this, I lose You - yet no true thought of Who I lose, rather fear of hell and (of being) shut out from Heaven."*[6]

Truly God was part of her life, but she didn't really know Who He was or what part He played in her day-to-day existence. As all the gifts she had been given were taken away, one by one, her mind and soul focused more clearly on the God in her life. She had taken God seriously, but had never taken any form of organized religion earnestly. She attended services at the Episcopalian Church; but she wore a Catholic crucifix! Her children were baptized Episcopalian, and yet she was greatly influenced by Calvinist philosophies, due, no doubt to her aunt's teaching her Huguenot errors when she was young. She believed in the Angels and longed for the peace of living in a cloister. The Bible was her constant companion all her life. At times of stress, she found consolation in the Word of God.

Elizabeth's gradual but steady walk towards the Lord was almost as if she knew how much she would need him in the years to come. As if her life had ever been joyful, with the exception

[5]Luke 12:34
[6]Mrs. Seton - Joseph Dirvin Pg 46

of those few years when she and Will Seton were first married, it
never got better, only worse. One of her greatest sorrows was
the death of her father, Richard Bayley. Although he never
bequeathed anything material to her or her sister, in his later
years, he left his wife and the family he had sired with her, and
went to live on his own in Staten Island, but kept Elizabeth and
her family around him as often as possible. She and he
developed a relationship she had always wanted, playful father
and daughter banter, especially in their letter-writing.

He had become a one-man defender of New York City
from plagues and Yellow Fever. However, he was not immune
to the vicious attack he had seen others die from. It took his life
in a very painful way. He had to have his daughter by him, the
one he loved most, until the very end. This was an extremely
difficult time for Elizabeth. But she found a great deal of solace
from her spiritual director, Reverend Hobart of Trinity Church on
Wall Street. They became very close, spiritually. He brought her
to a greater understanding of how God was working in her life
and that of her family. He explained how her struggles and
suffering, of which she had more than her share for her young
twenty-six years, were the Lord's way of purifying her in
preparation for her role in the church.

Elizabeth began evangelizing to her family and friends.
She knew her husband's time was short. He had been a Christian
in name only. He still embraced the Deist philosophy that God
really had no part in his life. She had to bring him into full
communion with the Lord. Remember now, she's working as a
Protestant, and Episcopalian, not as a Catholic. But she was very
strong converting her husband and instilling a genuine love of
God in her children. This was not an easy task, as their family,
as well as most of the Setons and Bayleys, had never given God
more than Sunday lip service. Now Elizabeth was attempting to
have them accept God as the center of their lives.

Soon on the heels of the death of her father, came the
downfall and destruction of her own husband, her Will, friend

and lover of her young years. He was completely crushed when his business fell apart. Even then he was showing signs of consumption, a precursor to Tuberculosis, from which his father had died. Will's illness took a few years before it completely incapacitated him. However, by the Spring of 1803, she knew that something had to be done. That summer, Elizabeth and Will made what everyone considered a very rash decision to sail to Italy, to visit friends he had made during his importing days, Antonio and Amabilia Filicchi. While Elizabeth knew that nothing was going to save her husband, they both sincerely believed the sea air and change of climate might heal him, or at least make his last days more peaceful. To this end they made the voyage, taking with them their eldest daughter, Anna, eight years old, leaving the rest of the children with other relatives.

They set sail in October 1803, and at first it seemed as if the tonic was working. Will showed a great deal of improvement. The journey took close to seven weeks, which gave Elizabeth and Will an opportunity to get some well-deserved rest, especially after the last few dreadful years. For the most part, the trip was beautiful, with just a few storms along the way breaking into their peace. Elizabeth and Will became closer to each other than they had ever been, and closer to the Lord. Elizabeth was able to read from Scriptures, and share about the good God with Will, and how He loved them. Will was coming along beautifully.

By the time the ship pulled into port at Livorno (or Leghorn), in the Tuscany area of Italy, the little pilgrimage of three were ready to leave the ship and take advantage of the hospitality they knew their friends, the Filicchis were planning for them. This was when the nightmare began. What they hadn't considered was the Italian government's fear of the spread of the deadly disease, Yellow Fever, which had claimed the lives of so many in New York, including Elizabeth's father. Theirs was the first ship to bring the news of the Yellow Fever in New York. They would have to be quarantined in a dreadful place, damp and cold, for a month.

No one believed that Will would weather the long quarantine period. He went from ill to near death in that period of time. Elizabeth prayed throughout the ordeal for many things, for a healing of Will's body to a healing of his soul. She prayed that he would not die in this dreadful place in full view of his little daughter, who would be traumatized by it. She prayed for Heaven for her husband. She just prayed. Will and Anna prayed with Elizabeth. They passed each day as a gift from the Lord, and looked forward to the next. Meanwhile, the Filicchis brought them food whenever possible and tried to make the hell they were experiencing more bearable.

Finally, after one month, December 19, 1803, they were released. Will was more dead than alive. He had to be carried out from his confinement. They were brought to beautiful lodgings which the Filicchis had arranged in Pisa on the river Arno. All of this had been so romantic in the planning stages. It would have been so romantic now under other circumstances. But for Elizabeth, her focus was to make her husband comfortable for whatever time he had left. She did not look for a healing of the body. She thanked the Lord for what He had given her and her Will, these last weeks together. Other than those early years when they first began setting up house on Wall Street, this was the only time which was truly theirs. It was not the best of times, but it was all the Lord gave them. They took it.

During his last agony, Elizabeth watched over him the entire time. She spoke to him gently. When it seemed he might be having trouble, she asked, *"You feel, my love, that you are going to the Redeemer?"* She had to be sure he was not battling with the evil one at the moment of death. He finally answered her with a smile, "Yes." On the morning of December 27, 1803, two days after Christmas, eight days after being released from confinement, Will Seton, husband and best friend of Elizabeth, father of their children, went to his reward. The Lord had prepared him through his wife. Elizabeth was twenty-nine.

✟✟✟

Thus begins Elizabeth's walk to the Catholic Church. At the death of her husband, Elizabeth symbolically shed her former life and began to don the cloak of the Sisters of Charity, although it would be a little over five years before that would become a reality. We believe that everything Elizabeth Seton did in her life was a preamble to the time she would begin the first *free Catholic school* in the United States and her community of sisters in Emmitsburg, Maryland. We believe that Elizabeth Seton's life was packed full, because the Lord had so much to accomplish in such a little time. The next few years would be as joyful and sorrowful as her previous twenty-nine. It began with her mourning period. Actually, the Lord did not allow her a period of mourning. That time in quarantine and the eight days following were as much mourning time as Elizabeth could be allowed. The Lord had too much work for her to do.

In keeping with the Lord's plan, Elizabeth had no place to go after the death of her husband other than to the home of the Filicchis. They brought Elizabeth and Anna to their home after Will's funeral. They went so far beyond the norms of friendship, that even little Anna was to remark to Elizabeth, "Oh Mama, how many friends God has provided for us in this strange land! For they are our friends before they know us."[7]

Out of the mouths of babes.....This was so true. The Filicchis were really her husband's friends. Filippo Filicchi, the older of the two, had met Will through his father, William Seton Sr. Filippo had been in the United States on business, being in the same business as the Setons, the Import-Export business. Then Will Jr. went to Italy with Filippo in 1788 to learn about the Import-Export business. The following year, Filippo returned to the United States to marry an American girl, Mary Cowper. The friendship continued through the Seton's difficult times, and it was an open invitation from the younger brother, Antonio and his

---

[7]Mrs. Seton - Joseph Dirvin Pg 128

Left:
***Statue   of   St.
Elizabeth   Ann
Seton   at   Seton
Shrine   Center,
Emmitsburg,
Maryland***

Above: ***This chapel, located on the grounds of Seton National Shrine
Center, held the remains of St. Elizabeth Ann Seton until 1962.***

wife Amabilia to the Setons which brought them to Italy on what became the occasion of Will's death. They embraced Elizabeth and Anna immediately. They were so much more than friends; they were as saintly a family as the Lord ever put into Elizabeth's path. On that day, when Will was buried in the cemetery at Livorno, the Filicchis opened their home and their hearts to the two Americans orphans, taking over the care of Anna so that Elizabeth could have time by herself to grieve the loss of Will.

The Filicchis and Elizabeth were evangelizing to each other. By the actions of both families, it became so obvious that God was the center of their lives. However, the Filicchis believed that Elizabeth was chosen to be a Catholic, and a strong Catholic at that. They believed that she loved God, and should be brought into the fullness of the Faith. Elizabeth believed that she already was in the fullness of Faith. And that's where the challenge began.

The Filicchis would never take advantage of a woman in grief and alone in the world. But to be the Filicchis, the people whom Will and Elizabeth had come to love before this tragedy struck, they had to be who the Lord had made them and that included talking to Elizabeth about the Faith. On a tour of Florence, in an effort to get Elizabeth's mind off her situation, they entered a beautiful church *La Santissima Annunziata,* the Holy Annunciation. No sooner had Elizabeth entered through the doors and the curtain separating the Sanctuary from the vestibule, the visual and audio ambiance of the Church made her fall to her knees in tears, happy that she was in the House of the Lord. It's not that Protestant churches don't reflect God, but the Catholic churches so reflect God, for a stranger, the impact is breathtakingly overwhelming. Everything about this church appealed to her senses, physical as well as spiritual. The paintings, the statues, the atmosphere of prayer, all of it shouted out *Church*; it was something she could not even describe. She had been used to the bare walls of Trinity Church in New York, but this was something that hit her deep in her soul.

She was aware that the Filicchis were trying to convert her, and it flattered her to a degree. But in her conscious mind, she was just being polite. She was not allowing their efforts to have any effect on her spirituality, and yet God was touching her gently, through these dear people. She was anxious to go home. She had spent this month of January, 1804, the month after her husband's death, with the Filicchis, and she had feelings of longing for home, mixed with the excitement she felt when she spoke to the Filicchis or the priest they sent over to convert her, as well as when she was in their churches. The Lord threw a monkey wrench into her plans to go home. The captain of the ship, the same one which had brought her over on her ill-fated journey with Will, told her the ship would not be ready at the end of January as had been scheduled. Rather, it would take another month to make the journey home.

When Amabilia told her, during Mass on Candlemas Day[8] that Jesus was truly present in the Blessed Sacrament and on the Altar, Elizabeth put her face in her hands and cried. This knowledge, and her hunger for the Bread of Life, was a direct cause of her conversion. This was the beginning. A week or so later, since the trip home had been postponed, they went for a day pilgrimage to a shrine of Our Lady of Grace, in Montenero, high above the ground, giving the pilgrim a panoramic view of the Mediterranean and the Alps. She attended Mass with the ladies. During the Consecration, as the Host was raised, a brash English tourist said to her mockingly, *"This is what they call their Real Presence!"*

Elizabeth went down on her knees in awe. The Lord had touched her where she could not resist Him, in her hunger for Jesus. The walls which she didn't even know she had put up, collapsed and she was naked before the Lord. In her own words:

---

[8]February 2 - At that time, it was the Feast of the Presentation of the Blessed Virgin Mary - in today's church, it is the Feast of the Presentation of Our Lord Jesus.

"My very heart trembled with shame and sorrow for his unfeeling interruption of their sacred Adoration; for all around was dead silence, and many were prostrated. Involuntarily, I bent from him to the pavement, and thought secretly on the word of St. Paul, with starting tears, `They discern not the Lord's Body' and the next thought was, how should they eat and drink their very damnation for not discerning it, if indeed it is not there? Yet how should it be there? And how did He breathe my soul in me? And how, and how a hundred other things I know nothing about?"[9]

Elizabeth kept all these things in her heart, but her focal point was her home in New York and her family. That's all her mind could handle at this point. She had been touched deeply by the Lord, but she was frightened. She had to sort things out. She was grateful to the good God when her ship sailed in February. However, the Lord wasn't ready for her to go back in her confused state. Anna came down with Scarlet Fever. They were taken off the ship and back to the Filicchi's home. Anna convalesced for three weeks at which time Elizabeth came down with Scarlet Fever. They stayed there for another two months, finally setting sail on April 8, 1804 for the United States.

There was a very important reason for this. Something which Elizabeth had done all her life, she criticized Catholics for doing. From the time her little sister Kitty died, soon after her mother had died in childbirth of Kitty, Elizabeth would look at the clouds, praying that her mother and Kitty would peek out from those clouds and console Elizabeth in times of stress and sorrow. She prayed for her mother's intercession all her life. Yet, she, like so many Protestants, criticized us for praying to *our mother*, our Mary for her intercession. She wrote many of her experiences and feelings down for her step-sister, Rebecca Seton to analyze with her. About this, she wrote:

"A little prayer-book of Mrs. F(ilicchi)'s was on the

[9]Mrs. Seton - Joseph Dirvin Pg 136

*table, and I opened a little prayer of St. Bernard (of
Clairvaux) to the Blessed Virgin, begging her to be our
Mother, and I said to her, with such a certainty that God
would surely refuse nothing to His Mother, and that she
could not help loving and pitying the poor souls He died
for, that I felt really I had a Mother - which you know my
foolish heart so often lamented to have lost in early days.*

*"From the first remembrance of infancy, I have looked,
in all the plays of childhood and wildness of youth, to the
clouds for my mother; and at that moment it seemed as if I
had found more than her, even in the tenderness and pity of
a mother. So I cried myself to sleep on her heart."*

She also wrote to Rebecca of her amazement at how the
Filicchis observed fasting. "Why Rebecca, they believe all we do
and suffer - if we offer it for our sins - serves to expiate them.
You may remember when I asked Mr. H(obart) what was meant
by fasting in our prayer book - as I found myself on Ash
Wednesday morning saying so foolishly to the Lord *'I turn to
you in fasting, weeping and mourning.'* and I had come to church
with a hearty breakfast of buckwheat cakes and coffee... You
may remember what he said about its being *old customs etc."[10]*
But Elizabeth told Rebecca that the Filicchis actually fasted
before receiving Communion. She told her how during Lent,
Mrs. Filicchi did not eat at all until after 3 p.m. every day.

By the time she was prepared to return to New York,
Antonio and Filippo, as well as a priest who had volunteered to
work with Elizabeth, loaded her down with various books on the
authenticity of the Catholic Church. Many of the points in these
books came from Holy Scripture, as well as the Episcopalian's
own *Book of Common Prayer*. For her part, Elizabeth was
almost converted before she set foot on the ship. But there was
that small doubt, and Elizabeth was not the kind of person to go
into something if she didn't believe in it totally. We don't know

---

[10]Mrs. Seton - Joseph Dirvin Pg 138

what pressures she anticipated upon returning to a completely Protestant world. But the two Italian evangelists, Antonio and Filippo, as well as their wives, feared what tension would be put upon her at home by her Protestant family, Protestant friends and her pastor, Protestant Reverend Hobart. As an extra added precaution, it was decided that Antonio Filicchi would accompany Elizabeth to New York, for moral support, and in the event she needed his financial help. However, that was a road Elizabeth did not want to travel. Their fears were well-founded.

Her first shock upon disembarking from the ship was that Rebecca, her step-sister, whom she called her soul sister, was not there to greet her. Indeed, she was dying in her room. She was the one to whom Elizabeth had written what she termed the Leghorn Chronicles, all her thoughts and questions which she had to funnel through Rebecca. In addition to losing her very best friend in all the world, she was losing her confidante. Rebecca tried to listen to Elizabeth as she shared what had happened to her, but the dear child was so close to death, she could do nothing but pray for Elizabeth in her struggle. Rebecca died within a few weeks of Elizabeth's return to New York. It was tragic for Elizabeth.

Elizabeth immediately announced to family and friends that she was investigating the Catholic Church with an eye towards joining it. At first, her friends rushed to her side, trying to talk her out of what they believed to be impetuous behavior. But they knew really nothing about their Faith, much less the Catholic Faith. In anger, most of them disassociated themselves from Elizabeth. Part of this group was her family, who were all card-carrying Episcopalians; not necessarily practicing Episcopalians, but members of the church. Elizabeth needed these people for help in financing a place to live and in the upbringing of her five children.

It was extremely difficult for Elizabeth, in that she had never had to beg before, especially from family. If the truth were to be known, she had always been the one to help other members

of the family. Her father had put *this one* through medical school
and got him started in private practice. Her father-in-law helped
that one begin in business, and he was doing very well.
Elizabeth had always been available to help anyone at any time,
and now she found herself asking for handouts. She was able to
get just enough to take care of herself and her children in the
most meager fashion. But it was an ongoing struggle.

Her biggest spiritual hurdle was Reverend Hobart. He had
been her spiritual advisor, her mentor, her friend in Christ. Now
she found herself on opposite sides of the fence from him. He
didn't know how learned Elizabeth had become in the time she
had been away from New York. So he began on a simple basis.
When her knowledge of Theology proved to be far beyond that,
he gave her books which would counter-attack the books she had
been given by Filippo Filicchi and the priest. This served to
confuse and anger her. It was one thing to counter a truth she
had read in Francis de Sales *"Introduction to a Devout Life"* and
some of the other Apologetic books given her; but when the
books insulted the Church and called Catholics heretics who
would join the Pope in the bottomless pit of hell, and when her
Reverend Hobart proclaimed that the Catholic Church was
corrupt, that was about as much as she could take.

She went back and forth, like a Ping-Pong ball. First, she
would read something in favor of the Church as a truth, possibly
from the Council of Trent. Then she would read Protestant
propaganda contradicting what she had read from Catholic
resources. Who and what should she believe? One thing is sure,
however, she never gave up on God. She was having problems
with some of His people on earth, but she knew that God loved
her and would lead her where He wanted her.

She distanced herself from the Episcopalian church, but at
the same time she did not go to the Catholic Church, unless it
was with Antonio. She prayed with her children, and somehow
the Hail Mary would find its way into their prayers, as well as
many Catholic devotions. She would pass by Catholic Churches,

lingering, trying to work up enough courage to go in, because that's where she truly wanted to be. But she was concerned also for her children. She didn't enjoy being ostracized by her former friends, but she could not bear to see her children hurt in any way. She was worried about them; would they be snubbed by the children of former friends of their mother, and why? What did they do?

This was truly the *Dark Night of the Soul* for Elizabeth Bayley Seton. She lived for months with attacks coming from all sides. She had to be alone. She separated herself from everyone and everything except the Lord. Towards the end of 1804, after almost a full year of should I, shouldn't I, from the time the Filicchis had begun to draw her into the Catholic Church, she finally broke. She described it to the wife of Antonio Filicchi, Amabilia. She shared how out of desperation, she became bold with the Lord.

"Would you believe, Amabilia, in a desperation of heart I went last Sunday to St. George's (Catholic) Church.

"...I looked straight up to God and I told Him: `Since I cannot see the way to please You whom alone I wish to please, everything is indifferent to me; and until You do show me the way You mean me to walk in, I will trudge on in the path You suffered me to be born in, and go even to the very Sacrament where I once used to find you.'

"...But if I left the house a Protestant, I returned to it a Catholic, I think, since I determined to go no more to the Protestants...

"...it finished calmly at last - abandoning all to God - and a renewed confidence in the blessed Virgin...

"...Now they tell me: take care, I am a mother, and my children I must answer for in judgment, whatever faith I lead them to.

"...That being so - I WILL GO PEACEABLY AND FIRMLY TO THE CATHOLIC CHURCH..."[11]

On March 14, 1805, she made her profession of Faith to the Catholic Church, accepting all the doctrines of the Council of Trent.

On March 20, 1805, Elizabeth made her First Confession. She stated it to be one of the greatest experiences in her life. She exclaimed *"It is done! Easy enough: the kindest, most respectable confessor is this Mr. O (Father O'Brien) with the compassion and yet firmness in this work of mercy which I would have expected from Our Lord Himself."*

On March 25, 1805, Feast of the Annunciation, she received First Holy Communion. This is the date given as the date of her entrance into the Catholic Church. She said of this occasion for which she had waited for over a year, *"At last, Amabilia, at last, GOD IS MINE AND I AM HIS! Now let all go it round - I HAVE RECEIVED HIM."*

✝✝✝

Now what? Elizabeth had in effect married the Catholic Church. She had embraced everything Mother Church taught, and accepted the articles of Faith as handed down by the Council of Trent and all the Councils over the last 1800 years. She prayed the Nicene Creed as we would say the Pledge of Allegiance to the United States when we were a patriotic country. Everything should have been wonderful. All her troubles should have ended. She had made the right decision. But they weren't. As a matter of fact, things could not have been worse for Elizabeth Seton, Catholic. She had lowered her social status. Catholicism was the Faith of the maids and servants, street people, immigrants, God yes, so many immigrants.

Catholicism was not the Faith of the genteel, members of the social strata of New York City. We must remember, this was not and is not now a Catholic country. Catholic bashing has been

---

[11]Mrs. Seton - Joseph Dirvin Pg 163

a sport for centuries in this country. Some of the founding fathers, people in our country whom we have always admired, were anti-Catholic. Names from the history books, Thomas Jefferson, Samuel Adams, and on and on were definitely not sympathetic to Catholics. John Jay, who wrote a Naturalization Law, stated that *no one could hold political office unless he renounce allegiance even to foreign ecclesiastical powers.* Well, what did they consider the Pope, but a foreign ecclesiastical ruler?

Elizabeth found herself in this category, considered an agent of a foreign power; she, whose family names of Bayley and Seton had been architects of the New York culture, and therefore, the American culture. What a disgrace this was. Even her family and friends spoke to her patronizingly, as if to a child at best, and disdainfully at worst. Now, something we have not mentioned up to this point is Elizabeth's trigger temper. She had the ability to go ballistic in an instant. She had worked all her life to control it, considering it a shortcoming and luxury for a lady of her standing to give vent to hot anger. Especially during the period when she was investigating the Catholic Church, she maintained her composure many times when she wanted to level a torpedo blast at an opponent. But she did not, wherever possible.

However, now that she had taken the plunge into *enemy territory*, the gloves were off with many people who just wanted the freedom of cutting her, using her conversion to Catholicism as a good excuse. Most of the time Elizabeth bit her tongue and other times parried with them, barb for barb. But 'there were some times when it went beyond playful antagonism, where she let her ire vent itself on her opponents. Usually her attackers were no match for Elizabeth and shrank back to wait for a more opportune time to get her. Very often, knowing they were no match for her, they would find other ways to stick the sword into her back.

But all of this was a sincere hurt on the part of Elizabeth

Seton. She had been so good to these people. She could not believe that they could not only abandon her at this time, but be so bitter and callous about it. And some of the reasoning defied logic. She hurt Uncle so-and-so's feeling. He was deeply offended by her conversion. It was as if by cutting her and her new-found religion, they could get her to abandon her *lunacy* and come back home to the Episcopalian or any Protestant religion for that matter. Anything would do other than Catholic. Elizabeth kept saying to Antonio Filicchi, *"It's not an option. I tell them instantly, with a cold, decided countenance that the time of reasoning and opinions is past."*

In addition to her problems with her religion, or perhaps because of them, she was having many problems trying to support her family. It had been planned that she would tutor and board the children of John Wilkes and his brother Charles, plus a number of others in the area. She had been living in a house owned by John Wilkes since her return from Europe. She could continue to live there and this would be a way for her to earn some income. With her conversion to Catholicism, this plan soured because all the children involved were Protestant, and the parents feared that this new zealous convert would try to sway their children towards her religion. The plan was put on the back burner for a time, and then dropped entirely.

Once that happened, Elizabeth knew she had to get another house for her family to live in. An offer came from a well-meaning man and his wife for Elizabeth to take his children and hers, and open a school for girls and boys in Manhattan. He would provide the house for the school. Her rent would be paid and her children would receive their education without charge. At first it seemed like it would work. She was really excited about it. Then her former mentor, Reverend Hobart tried to convince all the parents that her benefactors were Catholic, and between Elizabeth and this husband and wife, Mr. and Mrs. White, they were going to take all their children away from their Protestant roots.

They were able to convince him that this was not so. The White couple were Protestants and the school was meant to be secular, not religious. So the Reverend Hobart removed his objections and the school went ahead. But the die had been cast. The seeds of doubt had been sewn. They were never able to get more than a few children into the school and after less than three months, the project failed. Elizabeth had to get out of this house, and so her sister Mary and brother-in-law Wright Post, moved her and the children into their home in Greenwich Village which was a lovely neighborhood in 1805.

Things were not working out too well with her sister. Elizabeth attributed it to the fact that she had converted. Others maintained it was because they were sisters and had always had disagreements. The Catholic thing only accelerated the problems. One of the major problems with her Catholicism was the eating of fish, which at that time, was required not only on Friday, but Saturday also. Obviously, fish was an expensive luxury in those days as it is today, and not that many people liked fish, as they do not today. The problem was solved by the local priest, Fr. O'Brien who gave Elizabeth a dispensation from eating fish on Friday and Saturday.

She was able to get a house of her own when John Wilkes revived his original plan to have Elizabeth board his children and other children without mothers. This time it was under the supervision of a Protestant who had the school which they would attend, and so as soon as they could convince everyone that Elizabeth was not about filling the little minds with Catholic doctrine, the plan went into effect. She worked very hard, and things seemed to be taking on a good turn for her and her family.

That is, until her step-sister Cecilia Seton, child of Will's father, William Seton Sr., became completely enamored with the Catholic Faith. Originally, she and two other girls, Harriet Seton and Eliza Farquhar were passionately in love with everything Catholic and wanted to join the Church. The other two backed out when the pressure from Protestant society got to be too much.

However, Cecilia, much like her sister Rebecca, was Elizabeth's protégé, and very strong in her beliefs.   She may have been influenced by Elizabeth, but the Holy Spirit had been her greatest source of inspiration. But when the girl converted to Catholicism, the whole community blamed Elizabeth, and the hate campaign which had plagued her for a year and a half when *she* converted, began all over again, only this time with a vengeance.

Elizabeth was truly the innocent victim, but she was made to pay a high price for her Faith. Cecilia was thrown out of her home and disowned by her brothers and sisters. Remember, the parents were long dead; Elizabeth had reared the seven children for some time. These same children were now the ones who were attacking her over the conversion of their other sister, Cecilia. Elizabeth and her family were written out of wills by wealthy relatives who previously had made her their sole heirs. She could not afford to let this happen, but she could not betray her new convert, Cecilia. So while she prayed to be able to handle this cross, it was perhaps the most difficult time in a life which had always been difficult, at best. Her friend, Antonio Filicchi, had returned to Italy. Another friend, Fr. Tisserant, had returned to Europe with Antonio. Most of her support system was not within reach at a time when she needed them most.

She might have been able to handle this situation better if it had not been for her children. They had not asked for this. They had followed their mother into the Catholic Church, but they had not been given any choice as to whether they wanted to suffer the persecution which came naturally, being the children of Elizabeth Ann Seton. The children in the boarding house began to ridicule her and behave insolently. The parents, who had goaded the children into this behavior, blamed Elizabeth. All of them made fun of her in plain sight of her children. She may have been at the lowest point in her life. It was time for the eleventh hour God to take charge of the situation. And take charge, He did.

The End of the Beginning

The Lord sends His big guns to take over. Before Antonio had left for Italy, he had investigated two areas for the Seton boys to attend schools. One was in Montreal, Canada, to which he was partial. The other was Georgetown University or St. Mary's in Baltimore, Maryland, to which Elizabeth was partial. She had come under the wing of Archbishop Carroll, the first archbishop in the United States. Although they had never met at this point, he corresponded with her over the years, advising her as much as possible. He even offered to help with the cost of the boys' education at Georgetown. Elizabeth felt this was the Lord's Will.

The archbishop and Elizabeth finally did meet in May, 1806. Elizabeth shared with him her "secret," a longing she had for years which she never stated openly to anyone; she wanted to live the life of a religious in a convent where she could teach. The archbishop gave her a special gift; he gave her a week's instruction in preparation for her reception of the Sacrament of Confirmation. She was thrilled with this, not only the honor of having the archbishop give her this personal attention, but to receive the gifts of the Holy Spirit. On May 26, 1806, she was confirmed, taking the name Mary as her Confirmation name. From that time forward, she asked to be called Mary Elizabeth Ann Seton. She had it all, the Mother of God, the cousin of God and the grandmother of God, the mother of Mary. Archbishop Carroll addressed all her correspondence from that time on to Mary Elizabeth Ann Seton.

In November of that year, 1806, the Lord sent a special "*can-do*" priest to Elizabeth, Fr. William Dubourg. Elizabeth shared her "secret" with Fr. Dubourg, her desire to live the religious life and teach young girls. The priest, who was one to make up his mind immediately, agreed that she should do that, but did not think she should wait until her boys had graduated school. He suggested that she begin immediately. He took her by surprise, but she felt he was speaking the Word of the Lord to her. We get the impression that he was ready to ship her off within an hour. However, he was not that impulsive. She had spoken of the possibility of going to Montreal in Canada, where there was a larger population of Catholics than New York, and where she would probably be well-received. He went to Boston to confer with other priests who knew of Elizabeth, Fr. Cheverus and Fr. Matignon.

Two weeks later, he returned and suggested Baltimore rather than Montreal. The fact that her sons, James and William were nearby, was an added incentive for her. She asked what Archbishop Carroll thought of the idea. Although he had been ill for six months, and was not familiar with any of the particulars of the plan, he respected Fr. Dubourg and the two priests in Boston, Fr. Cheverus and Fr. Matignon. Fr. Matignon told her the following: *"You are destined, I think, for some great good in the United States, and here you should remain in preference to any other location."*.[12] That has proven to be a major prophecy.

Elizabeth Ann Seton was never one to run *from* something, rather than running *to* something. The offer to relocate to Baltimore was a firm one, and it was definitely what she planned to do, when the time was right. But there were situations which had to be resolved. She would not have left New York, because of the persecution she had been subjected to, as a result of Cecilia's conversion. She felt a responsibility to Cecilia also, to be there for her, supporting her as long as the Lord saw fit. However, Cecilia did follow her to Baltimore and joined her community.

She also had the obligation to the head of the school, who had given her the opportunity to board the children of John Wilkes and others at a time when she was destitute. She would not leave him as long as he needed her. But her heart was not in her birthplace anymore. She would always hold New York dear to her heart as the site of so many joys, including, but not limited

---

[12]Mrs. Seton - Joseph Dirvin Pg 199

to her marriage, the birth of her children, the home of her father, the place of her conversion, her reception of First Holy Communion and Confirmation along with a thousand other things. But she could let go. It was up to the Lord.

When the Lord wants something done, He moves quickly. Her responsibility to the school was resolved in short order. The number of boarders dwindled, first to half, then to a handful. Elizabeth had to get a smaller house, which upset the parents. It was just a matter of time before that venture would be finished. Rather than be concerned about what she would do, she contacted Fr. Dubourg, who put the plan into motion which would prove to be the beginning of a major movement in the Catholic School system in this country, and the first religious order in the United States. All the pieces fell into place. The property was procured. Fr. Dubourg was able to get a group of girls, whom Elizabeth could board; the tuition of the boys at Georgetown would be taken over by Fr. Dubourg somehow, so that Elizabeth could use the funds that the Filicchi family had made available to her, for her new venture. Within an extremely short period of time after having made the decision, three weeks to be exact, on June 9, 1808, she boarded a ship to take her on her new adventure. Elizabeth Ann Bayley Seton became Mother Seton. She never looked back.

The Lord's plan went into action immediately. We must just comment on one breath of fresh air to which the Seton family was made recipients, when they first arrived in Baltimore. Everybody they met liked them! They were all friendly! When they went from the ship on a long carriage ride to their new home and chapel, the chapel was lit brightly. The bishop, all her priest friends, Fr. Hurley, Fr. Dubourg, his sister, and many well-wishers were there to welcome her and the children. The word had gone out all over Baltimore about the widow Seton and her family coming to open a school. The greatest effect was on the children. They felt wanted! These people were like they were! They were Catholic!

The home was more than they had dreamed possible. The little school began with seven girls and within a short period of time increased to ten, as much or more than Elizabeth could handle. She was beginning to feel the effects of all the years. She tired more easily; she was ill more frequently. Her children were concerned about her well-being. But she turned everything over to the Lord. Apparently the Lord's plan was not *just* to open the school, but to get moving on the religious community as well. Elizabeth had never been so bold as to consider herself the foundress or mother superior of a religious community. Her limited ambition was to live the life of a nun, while being able to teach children.

However, that was not the Lord's plan, nor was it the ambition of Fr. Dubourg and the other priests in Baltimore; nor for that matter, was it the ambition of Archbishop Carroll. They could all see the makings of a religious community under the leadership of Elizabeth Seton. Fr. Dubourg even had recruited two girls from Philadelphia, who wanted to go to Spain, most likely to become Carmelites. He talked them into waiting until Elizabeth had her house open, which he anticipated would be the fall of 1809. She didn't know how this was going to come about, but she left herself completely in the hands of the Lord, in this case, through Fr. Dubourg and Archbishop Carroll. Fr. Dubourg told her to keep repeating the Scripture passage, *"The barren woman shall be the joyful mother of children."* and while this did not strictly apply to Mother Seton, having borne five children, the point was well-taken and turned out to be another prophecy.

Elizabeth put herself completely in the hands of the Lord, who would decide what and when anything should happen. However, we believe the Lord turned most of it over to Fr. Dubourg, who determined that this was going to be an operational convent before the end of the year. To that end, he made up a set of preliminary rules. He advised Elizabeth to begin accepting young ladies into the community. He received her vows of religion, permitted her to adopt a habit, and gave her the title of Mother. The girls began arriving on December 8, 1808, but Elizabeth did not take her vows and receive her habit and title until March 25, 1809, Feast of the Annunciation, and exactly four years to the day from her entrance into the Catholic Church.

Mother Seton, Mystic?

We haven't spoken in this account of St. Elizabeth Ann Seton about any visions, locutions or mysticism. Quite honestly, that's because we haven't come across anything of that nature. And Mother Seton had always been a very down-to-earth, practical woman. However, the time was to come when the Lord would decide when the community would be built, where it would be built, and how it would be financed. And that information had to be projected to Mother Seton.

This question had been rolling around for some time in Elizabeth's mind. She even wrote to Antonio Filicchi in Italy, in an attempt borrow money for the building of the convent, but although her letter reached him, his reply never reached her. She took this as rejection at first, until a year later when his letter arrived, long after the fact. But it is obvious that she was throwing out feelers. Whoever the Lord wanted to be involved, would respond in a positive way. That was Elizabeth's thinking. However, the Lord unfolded another plan, His plan.

One day, Elizabeth ran into the office of Fr. Dubourg to tell him what the Lord had clearly said to her during Communion at Mass that day. *"Go and address yourself to Mr. Cooper; he will give you what is necessary to commence the establishment."* Now, this could be considered by some as being out of left field. Mr. Samuel Cooper was a well-to-do young man from Philadelphia who had converted to Catholicism, and was discerning if the priesthood was where the Lord wanted him. He met Elizabeth when Fr. Hurley brought him to Baltimore for the consecration of St. Mary's Chapel. They had become close friends for a while, because they had so much in common. They went their separate ways in their search for God's Will in their lives, but remained friends and were in communication with each other from time to time. They had not seen each other for a while, and so the suggestion had to come from the Lord; it didn't come from Elizabeth.

Fr. Dubourg agreed that this might be the Word of the Lord, but didn't want Elizabeth to pursue it any farther until the Lord had an opportunity to speak to Mr. Cooper's heart. By the Lord's coincidence, Mr. Cooper dropped in on Fr. Dubourg *that same evening*, asking what was happening with the convent for the ladies who wanted to embrace the religious life. Without mentioning anything about Elizabeth Seton to Mr. Cooper, he shared that there were many who wanted to proceed with this project, but they couldn't for lack of money. Mr. Cooper said to him quite calmly, *"I have ten thousand dollars which I can give you for this purpose."* Bingo!

Fr. Dubourg, who believed in Divine Intervention as well as the next man, was knocked from his seat. He asked, in an effort at calmness, *"Have you been speaking to Elizabeth Ann Seton?"* Mr. Cooper said he had not, but then asked if she would be considered as heading up the project. When Fr. Dubourg confirmed that, Mr. Cooper seemed very happy with the idea. Fr. Dubourg held him off for two months, in the event he wanted to change his mind. To the contrary, he was chomping at the bit to begin. He immediately became involved with the project of building a convent for the Sisters. He even prophesied where it would be located. When he brought the money to Fr. Dubourg, he said, *"Sir, this establishment will be made at Emmitsburg, a village eighteen leagues from Baltimore; and then it will extend throughout the United States."*

At the mention of Emmitsburg, the priest was taken aback. He did not really approve of the idea of being out of Baltimore. Neither did Elizabeth Seton; neither did the archbishop. Of all the people involved, only Mr. Cooper saw the vision of Emmitsburg, and while he vowed he would not exert any influence in choosing the location, Emmitsburg was the final choice.

Elizabeth wrote to Filippo Filicchi, apprising him what had happened, and now, rather than asking him for money to build the project, she invited him to be involved in any way he could with Fr. Dubourg and Mr. Cooper. In this letter to Filippo, she made an unusual revelation. The final proof for them that this was being done directly by the Lord was given to Elizabeth by Fr. Matignon, from Boston, who had befriended Elizabeth some years before. Elizabeth confided to Filippo Filicchi the following in a letter: *"Fr. Matignon had suggested Cooper's plan to Elizabeth long before Cooper himself had ever thought of it. It is no wonder that everyone concerned in the matter was profoundly convinced that the hand of God was writing on the wall."*

Progress came rapidly after this. As we mentioned previously, on March 25, 1809, Elizabeth took her vows of Poverty, Chastity and Obedience, was given the title of Mother Seton, and a habit was authorized. Four girls received the habit with her. They embraced the rule of St. Vincent de Paul, but modified it for the work they would be doing. They took the name of the Sisters of Charity of St. Vincent de Paul.

The girls flocked to the little convent way out in Emmitsburg. Where there had been fear that the distance from civilization would discourage some from coming, for Mother Seton it was excellent, in that it was a true departure from the world and all its wiles. She was happy for another reason as well. Her eldest, Anna, had fallen in love with a young man in Baltimore and it seemed like the courtship was going too fast. Elizabeth felt that the separation, however slight, might give both the boy and the girl some pause to consider what they were doing. But this was just an extra thank you to Jesus for giving them this beautiful place. The Lord must have felt it was the right place. It's been over 190 years and they're still there.

Mother Seton and the first group of sisters left Baltimore the beginning of June and arrived at their temporary home, Fr.

Dubois' home, at the parish of St. Joseph in Emmitsburg. It took a month before their little home was completed. Just prior to that time, the second group of Sisters of Charity came out, arriving towards the end of July. The official date of the move-in to their new home was the Feast of St. Ignatius of Loyola, July 31. Cecilia Seton, Elizabeth's step-sister, came and joined the community. Her sister, Harriet Magdalen Seton also joined. Many, many people came. The Lord was building community!

Thus the Sisters of Charity began their history in the Cumberland valley of Maryland. They had no teachers to tell them what was politically correct or incorrect in the protocol of running or belonging to a Religious Order. So the little band of Sisters, with the convert of four years who had never been a Sister, much less a Mother Superior made all kinds of mistakes and stepped on many toes. Some of their blunders were innocent and comical, resulting in a slap on the wrist from superiors who may have smirked at the humor of it. Other faults were of a more serious nature, even if they just flew in the face of protocol, but because of which the community was endangered of becoming extinct before it ever got off the ground. There were plots at given times to replace Mother Seton as superior in Emmitsburg and send her and a group of nuns to Baltimore, under the pretext of being concerned over her health.

The young Mother Superior and her wards cringed in the face of possible separation and division which could lead to severance of the group altogether. Elizabeth's greatest fear was that her community had been turned over to the Sulpician order to administer and supervise. None of the people, who had anything to do with the creation or formation of the community, seemed to have any say in their fate, including Archbishop Carroll. So she really had good reason to be concerned. The only denominator which no one seemed to figure into the equation was Faith in the Lord. He had a reason for bringing Elizabeth Seton this far in this short period of time, and He was not about to let people mess it up. The eleventh hour God came to the rescue as He always had, but in the process of making Elizabeth and the sisters wait until the last moment, He allowed them to learn how to behave in their new environment, whether right or wrong. And so they all learned together.

There were many attacks, which seemed like they would never end. The priest who had been put in charge of the community was determined either to get rid of Mother Seton, or to minimize her role to that of Foundress and baby-sitter. He tried everything he could to accomplish this end. One way he felt he could do this was to insist that the Sisters of Charity in the United States conform to the rule of the Sisters of Charity in Paris. Everybody held their breath until they received a copy of the rule of the Paris community. And with only one major exception, which could seriously jeopardize Mother Seton, the rules were identical.

The problem area was her ability to be superior while being responsible for the upbringing of her five children. This had always hung over her head. She had known it; the archbishop knew it; but this priest was sure he could use it to get rid of her. But the Lord would not let it happen! It was slow in coming; there were times no one was sure it would work out in Mother's favor. But through the efforts of the people of God, working, we believe, in direct cooperation with the Lord, it was resolved. When the community was to adopt the rules of the Sisters of Charity of St. Vincent de Paul of Paris in 1812, Archbishop Carroll modified the rule so that she could be the superior, although she had five children. He was truly her protector.

The Lord's other plan in the Elizabeth Seton, Sisters of Charity agenda was the creation of the Parochial School System in the United States. As the community of Sisters was being developed, on a parallel course, the Parochial School System was evolving. From the meager beginnings of widow Seton in New York, as mistress to a lot of boisterous children, to her teaching in the first school in Baltimore, the plan was developing and maturing. On February 22, 1810, the first three students from the parish of Emmitsburg, entered the Catholic school there, run by the Sisters of Charity. This was in effect, the beginning of the Parochial School System in the Untied States. Under the direction of Archbishop Carroll and Mother Seton, the Catholic Parochial school system soared and blossomed, bringing quality education to all Catholics in the country.

Illness, death and sadness were always part of Elizabeth Ann Bayley's life. They struck at Elizabeth Ann Bayley Seton's life with a vengeance, taking so many of her loved ones from her, including her father, her husband and children. Mother Seton was to see loved ones, step-sisters Cecilia and Harriet Seton die; her own daughter Anna, who became the first professed Sister of Charity before she died on March 12, 1812; and her youngest child and daughter, Rebecca, on November 3, 1816; Filippo Filicchi died the same year as Rebecca, 1816.

A tremendous blow came when her good friend and mentor, Archbishop Carroll, father of the Catholic Church in America, died on December 3, 1815. He had been such a powerful force in her life. It was he, whom Antonio Filicchi interested in the conversion of Elizabeth in 1804. He confirmed her in New York in 1806. He encouraged her to start the school on Paca Street in Baltimore. He administered her vows in 1809, but dispensed her from complete poverty because of her children.

It was hard. These people were so important to her. They were family of one sort or another. Her own children, whom she loved dearly, her half-brothers and sisters from her husband's father's family, her half-brothers and sisters from her father, Richard Bayley and his second wife, they had all formed the fabric of her life. To see them go was to see part of her own life leave her. But the Lord had prepared her for this. From that cold day in Pisa, Italy, when death visited her for the first time as an adult, as she buried her beloved husband, Will, little pieces of her were being taken away. It was as if when the time finally came for her to leave this earth, there would be nothing left to take. It would all be in Heaven, waiting for her.

Consumption, Tuberculosis. In Elizabeth's time, this disease was akin to Cancer today. The mere mention of TB struck fear into the hearts of those affected, and their loved ones. So many of Elizabeth's family and loved ones died of this dreaded disease. Her husband Will was the first to die of Consumption. His mother - Rebecca Curson Seton died of Consumption; as did her sister, Will's stepmother, Anna Marie Curson Seton; Elizabeth's daughter Anna Maria, and her dear friend and confidante, step-sister Rebecca; were stricken by the family disease; as was Elizabeth's step-sister Cecilia, who had joined her community, to be followed by her daughter Rebecca.

It was a family disease, which Elizabeth either contracted or inherited. She had always been in poor health. But the last few years seemed to be full of problems upon problems. There were always conflicts with the community, with those who would try to take the community away from her, or her from the community. There had been ongoing difficulties with her sons, who caused her much grief and probably served to intensify her illness. But while there was always work to do, new projects to begin and old projects to maintain, she had done the job the Lord had sent her out for; she had finished the race. At a very early age, only forty-six years old, Mary Elizabeth Ann Bayley Seton was ready to go Home. She missed so many people who had been important in her life. And although she anticipated a long stretch in Purgatory, she looked forward to being in Heaven with her Savior. She once wrote towards the end of her life: *"...could I hear my last stage of cough and feel my last stage of pain and the tearing away of my prison walls, how would I bear my joy? the thought of going Home, called out by His Will - what a transport!"*[13]

Mary Elizabeth Ann Bayley Seton died on January 4, 1821. She was forty-six years old. Her life was non-stop

---

[13]Mrs. Seton - Joseph Dirvin Pg 442

movement.

She was a faithful *daughter* - a loving *wife* - a loving *mother.*

She was an obedient *nun* - a strong *mother superior.*

She was a lover of Jesus in the *Eucharist* - a lover of *Mary.*

She is a *powerful woman* in our Church - a *role model* for today.

> She gave us the formula of her life:
>
> *"I am sick, but not dying;*
>
> *troubled on every side, but not distressed;*
>
> *afflicted, but not forsaken;*
>
> *cast down, but not destroyed;*
>
> *knowing the affliction of this life is but for a moment,*
>
> *while the glory in the life to come will be eternal."*

Thank you Mother Seton, for giving yourself to us. ***We love you!***

St. Paschal Baylon

Patron Saint of Eucharistic Conferences

St. Paschal Baylon is one of the most multi-faceted diamonds the Church has ever contained in its Treasury of Faith. He is a lay person, never having been ordained a priest. And yet he is the Patron of *Eucharistic Congresses* and *Confraternities of the Blessed Sacrament.* His whole life centered around the Eucharist, for which he is most known, and yet he would not become a priest. He felt only called to be a brother. He adored the Real Presence of Jesus in the Eucharist, but did not feel worthy to call Our Lord down onto the Altar as a priest of God.

For our purposes in this book, we want to track his *Journey to Sainthood.* He ranks high in the Communion of Saints, along with his peers Saints Dominic, Frances Xavier Cabrini, Elizabeth Ann Seton, Leopold, Angela Merici and all the Saints we're writing about in this Trilogy.[1] He is a Saint in whose path we could easily follow. But in order for you to understand his great contribution, in defense of the Real Presence of Jesus in the Eucharist, you must learn about St. Paschal.

He is virtually unknown in the United States, although there are a few churches named after him; one we know of in particular, is St. Paschal Baylon in Thousand Oaks, Southern California, the town next to Westlake Village, where we lived for twenty-five years. While we knew virtually nothing about him, all the years we were living next door to him, so to speak, imagine our surprise the first time we went to Lourdes; there in front of the Basilica of the Rosary was an altar, right next to St. Bernadette's altar, dedicated to St. Paschal Baylon, Defender of the Eucharist! There he was, clutching his hands together, clasped in an attitude of prayer, looking up to God the Father. How many Saints do you know who have their own altars in

---

[1] Read the trilogy of Super Saints: Book I - *Journey to Sainthood* - Book II - *Holy Innocence* - Book III - *Defenders of the Faith.*

Left:
**Saint Paschal Baylon was
named by Pope Leo XIII as
the Patron of Eucharistic
Congresses.
He is shown in adoration of
the Eucharist.**

Below:
**Statue of Saint Paschal
Baylon in the outside
chapel in front of the
Basilica of the Rosary in
Lourdes, France**

Lourdes? Not many! But this dear Saint Paschal, not well-known, and not even French, is right up there next to St. Bernadette.

Who is this Saint, this powerful brother in the eyes of God and the official Church, and yet practically unfamiliar to the whole world? Did the Lord put him in certain places, at a specific crucial time, because He knew that's where a man of Paschal's strength would be needed? He was a lay Franciscan in the Alcantarines, the community founded by St. Peter Alcantara, who died thirty years before St. Paschal. And yet Paschal was beatified before St. Peter. Keep in mind that nothing is done by coincidence in the Lord. If anything, we would have to call an occurrence Holy Coincidence. We want to share with you the life of St. Paschal Baylon, a simple, powerful Defender of the Eucharist and Defender of the Faith.

We can just envision the Heavenly Army of Angels descending on the little farm country of Torre Hermosa, (Beautiful Tower) Spain, in the month of Mary, May 15, 1540. Torre Hermosa is a short distance from Zaragoza, and the world famous Marian Shrine to Our Lady of Pilar,[2] where the people of Spain have been venerating Our Lady for the last two thousand years. Was Mary with the Angels that night? We know they were bringing a special gift to Martin Baylon and Elizabeth Jubeira - their son Paschal. He was a very exceptional child, born on Pentecost Sunday. His family were simple folk, shepherds. As good and holy parents, they taught their child in their humble way, all the beliefs of our Church that *they* had learned at the feet of their parents. Paschal grew up to love Our Lord Jesus, our Mother Mary and his Heavenly Family, our brothers and sisters - the Saints, and our cousins - the Angels.

Shepherding was a noble vocation which Paschal was to learn as a youth and adopt from the time he was seven years old,

---

[2]Read about the Shrine to Our Lady of Pilar in Bob & Penny Lord's book, *Heavenly Army of Angels*

until he reached the age of twenty-four. It was not because this was the extent of his ambition. Not at all. As a matter of fact, he taught himself to read and write, a major feat at that time. Keep in mind that the Gutenberg printing press had only been invented ninety years before the birth of St. Paschal, so reading and especially writing were not skills of which most people could boast, especially unpretentious folk, like shepherds. Most likely Paschal's parents could not read nor write, but their son had a great desire to learn the riches of our Church. So he did whatever it took to learn reading and writing. He may have had the help of the local priest, who could most likely read and write. *Or the Angels may have taught him.* We don't know for sure.

But he added this to the basket of goods he gathered to bring to the Lord. A paradox of sorts is, on the one hand, he worked very hard to better himself; and yet on the other hand, he contented himself with being a shepherd. Obviously it was not because he was lazy. There was a much greater reason, one which led Paschal all his life. The reason Paschal became a shepherd, and remained one until age twenty-four was basically out of *obedience* to his parents, who had a need for Paschal to be a shepherd to provide for their daily needs. So in the same positive way that he embraced everything in his life, and with the same zeal, he took up shepherding, and was the best possible shepherd.

He may have had some influence from Friars early on, because he wore garments very similar to those of a friar under his shepherd's outer garment. He walked barefoot, although it created great discomfort for him because of the rocky paths and bristles he had to cross over with his sheep. He didn't eat very much; he fasted whenever possible. He was actually living the life of a friar of St. Francis before he ever joined a religious order.

There were some inconveniences that shepherds have to live with. One of the most difficult for Paschal was not being able to attend Mass whenever he wanted. You can't just bring your flock to the local church and park them outside. No, his job as shepherd had to be treated as a vocation. But the Lord blessed his acts of obedience. You will be hearing much about that virtue, *obedience*, in this chapter on St. Paschal Baylon, as well as all the Saints who journeyed to the Kingdom on the rocky path. There is a classic tradition about St. Paschal regarding his difficulties attending Mass. His biographer, Fr. Ximenes, who knew him well, wrote of his early life, most likely from accounts that the young Paschal shared with him.

This particular account, shows Pascal Baylon's great love for the Eucharist, coupled with his trustworthy obedience to his job as shepherd. Actually, this account is also verified by an eyewitness, another shepherd who observed what happened. He saw Paschal Baylon kneeling in the fields, facing the sanctuary of Nuestra Señora de la Sierra, a distance away from where he was keeping his sheep. Paschal was immersed in prayer during the Mass. The eyewitness testified that Angels could be seen bringing the Blessed Sacrament suspended in the air over a chalice where Paschal was kneeling. He would spend hours venerating Our Lord Jesus in His Real Presence. According to the shepherd who was the eyewitness, this happened on more than one occasion. St. Paschal was in ecstasy at these times.

There are many traditions about St. Paschal which have been recorded by his biographer, Fr. Ximenes. St. Pascal had a very strong sense of justice, of right and wrong, and what his responsibilities were regarding things he judged wrong. A strong example of this was his attitude towards his flock. They were good; well-trained, but still they were animals. They wandered into the wrong places occasionally, and they chewed on vines and growing crops. They also trampled on grazing lands. Well, they had to. How else could they walk? The only problem was they were not trampling on his land! Paschal, being a shepherd, understood these things, but did not excuse the damage which might have been done to neighbors' lands and the responsibility for making restitution for the damages. He would very often give money to landowners, to make up for what he perceived was damage they had done to the landowners' lands. The landowners didn't expect it. Paschal's colleagues, other shepherds with whom he would associate, while they respected him greatly, thought this was a bit much, and resented the possible ramifications this might have on them and their sheep. They could just envision themselves having to pay penalties for damage their sheep would be responsible for. But Paschal was very firm in his thinking that the landowners had to be compensated.

During his years as a shepherd, he was looking beyond the horizon to where and how he wanted to spend his entire life. He ruled out things of the world at an early age. It is said he had visions of Sts. Francis and Clare of Assisi, in which they taught him many things. But as part of the visits they made to him, they also suggested he give his life over to God through the Friars Minor of St. Francis, or as we know them, the Franciscans. But even then, in considering the followers of Francis, wherever he would go and whatever he would do for the Lord had to be that much more. Like Father Francis, he always wanted to serve the Lord more than what might have been expected of a normal person. He wanted to give everything he had to Jesus and then some.

Towards the end of his teenage years, he began investigating various religious orders, mostly Franciscans. One of the communities of the Friars Minor he thought about was the Alcantarines, which had been founded by St. Peter of Alcantara, a Spanish Franciscan. Earlier in his life, St. Peter had been very influential on the life of St. Teresa of Avila. He helped her put into action, her reform of the Carmelite Order in Spain, which became the Discalced[3] Carmelites. While St. Peter gave much to St. Teresa during her most difficult times, he also learned much from her, with regard to reforming his own order, the Friars

---

[3]meaning without shoes

Minor, whom he believed had lost the vision which St. Francis and St. Clare had fought for most of their lives.

St. Peter started a community of Franciscans, which became later known as Alcantarines, after St. Peter of Alcanatara. It was austere. If it had been possible, it would have been more austere than the original rule of St. Francis of Assisi, and later, the Poor Ladies of St. Clare of Assisi, but nothing could have been more austere than those two communities.

This brotherhood of St. Peter of Alcantara, who was alive when Paschal first visited them, was about as severe as you could get. The only thing harsher than the rule itself was how the Friars tried to outdo each other in forms of penance and mortification. It was a one-upmanship society. One had to outdo the other. We pray it was all for the glory of God, rather than the pride of accomplishment, practicing the harshest penances and fasts possible. Paschal visited the community as a come-and-see candidate. He was about eighteen at the time. The brothers sized him up and determined he did not have what it would take to live this reform Franciscan rule. They rejected Paschal.

Perhaps this was good for young Paschal. He became determined that he was going to be accepted into that religious group. For the next six years, he prepared himself, both physically and spiritually, so that when the time came, after he reached his twenty-fourth birthday and was released from his responsibility of being a shepherd for the family, he went back to the Alcantarines with renewed vigor. He knew he was going to get in. It was like working toward getting an A+ on a test; if you're that type of person, you'll do whatever it takes to get the very best test results. And so at age twenty-four, he came back and was accepted into the community of St. Peter of Alcantara.

It did not take very long for the Franciscans of the Alcantarine reform to realize what a jewel they had in Paschal. He was truly a special person. They may not have actually known he was a Saint at the beginning; but after witnessing his behavior from the day he arrived at the monastery, his wellspring of virtues which sprang forth, they began to perceive the Saint in their midst. He excelled in possessing and practicing every virtuous quality known to the brothers at the time he entered the monastery.

For Paschal, he had arrived *home*. This was where the Lord wanted him to be, to shine, to set forth example for the other brothers, which they could then project to everyone with whom they came in contact. He was almost immediately made the *doorkeeper*. We have had some extremely powerful Saints and Blesseds who have attended the doors of monasteries and convents, waiting to welcome souls into their midst. Just to name a few, St. Bernadette of Lourdes was a doorkeeper, as was Blessed Sister Faustina and St. Martin de Porres, as well as Blessed Brother Andre of Montreal. There were many doorkeepers who have lined the halls of the Heavenly Kingdom. The Saints made it an opportunity to bring the love of Jesus and Mary, all the Angels and Saints to everyone with whom they came in contact. Very often, the doorkeeper was the first impression one had of the community.

He was a stickler for propriety. No one was above the rules of the Church. An example of this happened when he was doorkeeper. Some women came to ask the father guardian of the monastery to hear their confessions. Paschal told his superior, who then ordered him to tell the women that he was not there, but had gone out. Paschal said he could not do that; instead he replied. *"I will tell them that you are engaged in important matters."* The superior corrected him, "No, tell them that I am not at home." Paschal rose to his full height and spoke very low but definite. *"Forgive me, Father, I must not say that, for that would not be the truth and would be a venial sin."*[4] Then he returned to his post at the door. It's not stated exactly, but we believe the father guardian came down and heard the women's confessions.

---

[4]Butler's Lives of the Saints - Volume II -Pg 335

Paschal had a great love for the poor, the indigent and downtrodden. He did whatever he could, whenever he could to have special treats to give them. For himself, he asked virtually nothing, but he believed it was his responsibility to make the lives of the suffering as comfortable as possible, under the circumstances of their lives. He would pull all kinds of little tricks to get them a little something extra in the way of sweets, or dainty morsels.

As we told you at the beginning of our account of St. Paschal Baylon, he is known and has been known from the time he was alive, as a great lover of the Eucharist. This has been his claim to Sainthood; although we're not sure if his love of the Eucharist is what made him a Saint, or his saintliness made him such a lover of the Real Presence of Our Lord Jesus in the Eucharist. We do know that from the time he was a child, his focus in life was Adoration of the Blessed Sacrament. While he never let his other duties suffer, after his chores were completed and he could get away, you could find him in the chapel.

He opened the chapel in the morning and closed it at night. He served Mass after Mass whenever he was allowed. He would stay after everyone had left at night to retire, and adore Jesus in the Eucharist. There is a famous painting of him, showing how he would spend hours before the Blessed Sacrament. He was on his knees, kneeling straight up without any support, his hands firmly clasped together, above his head. He would maintain this position for hours, whether there were people watching or not. He did it for His Lord Jesus, not for the world. The expression on his face was always one of rapture.

Just for a moment, think about this position of St. Paschal Baylon, which he would keep for hours at a time. It's very difficult, especially when there is no support. And yet he did this often, very often. We would have to think under normal conditions that he would be in a great deal of pain or discomfort from maintaining this stance for such long periods. But he always had a look of joy on his face. It's almost as if he were not there in the chapel, but somewhere else. Could it have been Heaven?

A Spanish priest, other than Fr. Ximenes, wrote a biography of St. Paschal Baylon, many centuries ago. This was before he had been named Patron of Eucharistic Congresses; it was before there were such things as Eucharistic Congresses. The priest made the title of the book, *Vida del Santo del Sacramento S. Pascual Bailon.* In English it translates, *The life of the Saint of the Eucharist, St. Paschal Baylon.*

St. Paschal Baylon collected many prayers which he put into a makeshift scrapbook. Fr. Ximenes gives Paschal credit with having written these prayers. To have this collection of bits and pieces of writings, cut out, clipped in, all done by the Saint himself, is a beautiful tribute to our Saint. To know that these particular prayers touched his heart so tenderly that he wanted permanent records of them, to pass on to his brothers or possibly to commit them to memory so that he could share them while he was alive, this is what is important.

Originally, we wanted to put St. Paschal Baylon into the book on the Counter-Reformation, Defenders of the Faith, because of the battles he waged with the French Huguenots, but we decided that it was more important to focus on his journey to the Kingdom. However, we'd be doing you a great disservice if we didn't get into that aspect of his life. It's the only thing he did outside the monastery to glorify the Lord, and it almost cost him his life more than once.

Remember now, the time frame of the life of St. Paschal Baylon. He was born in 1540, seven years before the death of Martin Luther. All Luther's poison had been spewed on the Catholic population of the north of Europe, most especially Germany and the Scandinavian countries. His comrade-in-arms, John Calvin, who would do one better than Luther, took these heresies and spread them all over Switzerland, spilling over into France. The followers of Calvin in France were nicknamed Huguenots, which came from the German *Eidgenossen*, meaning conspirators. The Swiss pronunciation of the word was *eiguenotz*, meaning those rebelling against authority; in French it would sound like Hugenots. Whatever its origin, they were the most militant of the Sixteenth Century Protestants.

It's not known for sure why they sent Paschal Baylon into the fray. What they could have expected him to do in the heaviest concentration of Huguenots in France has not been determined. All that is known for sure was that he had to deliver a very important communication to Fr. Christopher de Cheffontaines, who was Minister General of the Observants.[5] Fr. Cheffontaines was located in the northwest of France, in Brittany. In order for Paschal to reach him, he had to go through the worst possible concentrated areas of the Huguenots, who were killing Catholics as much as looking at them. Possibly the worst thing Paschal could have done was to wear his Franciscan habit. But he was who he was. He never compromised himself. He would rather have died rather than deny who and what he was. He paid a high price for his loyalty to Church and Order. He was captured by Huguenots on more than one occasion. He was stoned a few times. However, we're told the second time, which could have been fatal, all the stones missed their marks by a wide margin. That was in all likelihood due to the Angels who were protecting him every inch of the way, blocking the stones from touching his body.

During this journey, he once was stopped by Huguenots in Orleans, France. Orleans was a hotbed of activity by Protestants and Catholics battling for control over the bodies and souls of the people and more importantly, the land they occupied. Taking control of major cities was an extremely important part of building their little kingdoms. The appearance of a habited Catholic friar did not do well for them, especially if the friar was

---

[5]Group of Franciscans who were permitted to follow more purely the original rule of St. Francis, which the Friars Minor and Conventuals felt was too primitive and austere.

as beautiful in spirit as Paschal Baylon. He was radiant when he spoke about Jesus. They had to put out that light. To that end, they questioned him about his belief in the Real Presence of Jesus in the Eucharist, most likely with an eye to tripping him up and then killing him.

However, the Lord just filled him with the Holy Spirit. He could not say anything wrong. We've got to remember that St. Paschal Baylon was not well educated. Although he taught himself to read and write, we don't read of any great amount of knowledge being accumulated by our Saint. So it had to be the Holy Spirit guiding him, in answering the questions. He not only did *not* fall into their trap, but he answered their questions so well and so in keeping with the teachings of the Catholic Church, many of them had tears in their eyes when he finished his dissertation on the Eucharist. There may have been some who converted. We know that many others wanted him killed, but another gift from the Lord was they did *not* kill him; they allowed him to live. He reminds us so much of St. Francis of Assisi, his father-in-faith, when he went among the Moslems. This pure love of Jesus and all things pertaining to his God surpassed their need to kill a Catholic and Franciscan friar at that. They were blinded by the light of Jesus they saw in his eyes, and coming from his lips. He had more than accomplished God's mission among the heretics.

However, he sustained serious wounds from the stonings which the Lord allowed to strike his body. Some of these bruises, he received from the rough treatment he was subjected to, had a lasting effect on his health. But he accomplished his mission, and was brought back safely to Spain. The Lord had a purpose for sending him into France. We think it had more to do with spreading the truths of the Church by his behavior and attitude than by any clandestine actions he might have considered with the French members of the Alcantarine movement. Perhaps the Lord wanted the Protestants, who had received such bad press about Catholics from their leaders, to take notice of this single gentle lamb, Our Lord Jesus was sending into their midst. There is a very popular expression among the students at Franciscan University in Steubenville. It is *"Preach the Gospel, and if you have to, use words."* We believe that is what St. Paschal Baylon was called on, by the Lord, to preach the Gospel without necessarily using words.

St. Paschal offered his entire life to Jesus in the Eucharist. He spent most of his time before the Blessed Sacrament. He was known as the Saint of the Blessed Sacrament. After his return from France, he spent the rest of his life in this simple way, adoring Our Lord Jesus in the Eucharist. His superiors knew he could do more for the movement in the Chapel, than in working among the brothers. While they wanted the other Franciscans in the community to have the gift of experiencing him, as the Lord had allowed the Protestants in France to, the Lord also wanted to experience him, and He came first.

So a compromise had to be struck. Brother Paschal would spend his time for the most part in the chapel. The brothers could find him any time they wanted, when he was off-duty from his various chores. He would be in the chapel in his famous pose, kneeling straight up with his arms above his head, in reverent adoration of his God. He became a great role model for the Franciscans in that community.

Paschal Baylon was born on Pentecost Sunday; he died on Pentecost Sunday 1592, at the Franciscan friary at Villareal. He was fifty two years old. As a special gift to Paschal, he was allowed to close his eyes for the last time just as the bell rang out the Lord's Presence during the Consecration of the Mass. He had just intoned the name of Jesus.

An avalanche of miracles began to occur almost immediately after he died. So many miracles were confirmed that the ecclesiastical authorities spared no time opening the cause for his Beatification and Canonization. He was officially beatified in 1618, twenty years after his death. This is unheard of, for anyone to be beatified so quickly. Even Saint Thérèse of

Lisieux took twenty-five years for her Beatification. Of course, she was canonized two years later, whereas St. Paschal Baylon was canonized in 1690. But still, that was a great honor paid to our little Spanish brother who never became a priest, and is still the patron saint of Eucharistic Congresses. He has been powerfully honored by his Church.

His main biographer Fr. Ximenes, who had been a minister provincial of the Alcantarines at one time in his priestly career, knew Paschal very well. He speaks with the highest praises for Brother Paschal. He was in different houses with him over the years, as well as on two different long trips. He stated,

"In no single case do I remember to have noted even the least fault in him, though I lived with him in several of our houses, and was his companion on two long journeys."[6]

St. Paschal Baylon never did anything dramatic or spectacular. Basically, he loved Jesus. He loved his Heavenly Family, and called on them often - all the Angels and Saints. He adored the Gift we've been given of the Blessed Sacrament in the tabernacle. In order to express that great love, he spent most of his time before the Blessed Sacrament in adoration. When the time came for him to enter into the Heavenly Kingdom, we can just picture Jesus at the head of the welcoming committee, followed by His beautiful Mother Mary, and then the Communion of Saints and Angels. Wouldn't you like that kind of welcoming committee when you go to the Father? I know I would. ***Praise Jesus!***

---

[6]Butler's Lives of the Saints - Volume II -Pg 335

Blessed Frederic

a priest and a dream

This story begins with a people, a loyal people who gave up all for Mother Church. Originally from France, the eldest daughter of the Church, till today they hold on to that heritage which made them great. Through over 300 years of persecution and bloodshed, the French Canadians have remained faithful to their Jesus, Mary and the Church.

This is more than a story of a Saint; it is the story of faith, determination, and zeal; it is the story of our Church. Our story begins in Cap de la Madeleine, once called *"a sandy mound not fit for man or beast."* This was man's poor assessment; God would show them that as a flower can bloom in the desert, a seed sown by men of faith can bring forth a jewel in a *"worthless sandy mound."* Here man, with little but faith, would bring to the North American continent a grand and magnificent Shrine, where hope and healings and consolation would be just some of the gifts received by the millions who come and venerate the Mother of God under the title of Our Lady of the Cape or as the French Canadians say, Notre Dame du Cap.

When Pope John Paul II came to the Shrine he said,

"Today, indeed, we come to Notre Dame du Cap as people of our time. We come with those generations of the past with whom we share our faith in the Mother of God. A fine inheritance has been bequeathed to you. It has made you what you are. And the cornerstone of that inheritance is Mary, to which your predecessors dedicated themselves. We are here to, as it were, transfer this sharing of faith into the hearts of our generation and their successors."

"Those generations of early witnesses provide us, who are here, with our inspiration. Intrepid (courageous) as the prophets, they generated faith, fanned it into flame, tended it lest it die out in the ashes of skepticism. When we are tempted to lose our grasp on hope, it is their faith in the future which

Left: ***Blessed Frederic Jansoone Apostle of Our Lady***

Above: ***Blessed Frederic arrives at Cap de la Madeleine on the St. Lawrence River.***

Above: ***Bridge built to commemorate the Miracle of the Ice Bridge at Cap de la Madeleine***

upholds and stimulates us. Through the generations it is the pilgrims' faith that confirms the special vocation of this Shrine."

"God's work born through suffering"

Before the magnificent spires rose from the Shrine of Cap de la Madeleine, as far back as the mid 1600's, when the first missionaries came and gave their lives for the Faith, pilgrims were already coming to a small church on this sandy mound, petitioning their Mother and then giving thanks for favors received. This Shrine was not something that just happened. Like any new birth, it was the fruit of love, between God the Father and the faithful of French Canada who produced this beautiful Shrine to Our Lady.

In the mid Seventeenth Century, Quebec was a French colony, settled by a people whose blood would nourish the Church through their martyrdom. Now, at that time, Cap de la Madeleine was a small, insignificant village with few inhabitants. Formerly just a stretch of sandy land, a French priest from Sainte Marie Madeleine (in France) gave it to the Jesuits to use for evangelization.

On September 8, 1634, Cap de la Madeleine received its first missionary, Father Buteux, a Jesuit who would later be martyred by the Iroquois on May 10, 1652. The first fourteen settlers were granted parcels of land to clear and cultivate. In 1659, the Jesuits granted the Boucher family, one of the first settlers, a small piece of land where they could build a chapel. There Monsieur Boucher built the first church in the Cap de la Madeleine and the faithful called it *The Church of Sainte-Marie-Madeleine.* In 1662, it was later moved onto the land where it now stands. After twenty-five years in the Cap de la Madeleine, the Jesuits left and the Franciscan Recollects took over in 1680.

The faithful of this area have always been strong prayer-warriors; when in need they invoked the aid of their Heavenly Mother, and She always honored that faith. The villagers received their first pastor October 14, 1685, and it was this priest, Father Vachon, who had only been ordained five short years, who began devotion to the Rosary at the Cap. He approached Rome for permission to set up the first *Brotherhood of the Rosary* in Canada; once begun, this movement swept all of French Canada.

As pastor, Father Vachon set up a Brotherhood of the Rosary Chapel in the first church in Cap de la Madeleine, placing a lovely silver statue on the altar.[1] By this time the modest chapel, built by Monsieur Boucher, was more than fifty years old and in need of much repair. Father Vachon's dream was to build a larger church, rather than repair the small chapel. After Monsignor de Saint Vallier, his superior, visited the tiny parish, Father received permission to build. Now, it was 1716; the parish consisted of sixteen families, with only eleven tithing in any way; in addition, there was little stone in the area that could be used for building.

Money was needed. Father Vachon started a fund-raising campaign which stretched beyond the Cap, far into the region. When the Bishop, Monsignor de Saint Vallier had seen the sad state of the little chapel that Monsieur Boucher had built, he appealed to both sides of the St. Lawrence River, where the Shrine is located, for help, adding he would donate some of *his* resources to the project. Work began on the new stone church, the summer of 1717. Volunteers came; they cleared the area of brush and trees,[2] dug the foundations and carried building materials - what little stones they could gather from surrounding fields. A new church of Sainte Madeleine began to rise. As the people laid the first cornerstone, had they had the slightest idea

---

[1] It was later stolen

[2] It reminds us of Mother Angelica and her Nuns, when they first arrived in Birmingham, Alabama, and began to build their convent in a state approximately 2% Catholic! The local Catholics all pitched in, clearing the land and providing help in every way they could; and what we see of the Monastery of Our Lady of the Angels today, is because one Nun made a promise to God, her Nuns followed her, and God sent angels to help her make it a reality.

what this would become, had they contemplated the growth of the Shrine someday and the multitudes who would pray there, they probably would have died of fright.

The Curé of Ars said, *"Leave a parish without a priest for twenty years and when you come back they will be worshiping animals."*[3] When Father Vachon died on March 7, 1729, the parish died with him; many moved to Montreal. As the village had not been greatly inhabited in the first place, it became what it had formerly been - a stop-over place, where a missionary would serve Mass on his way through. For more than a *century*, Cap de la Madeleine was without a priest!

Cap de la Madeleine receives a priest!

Although Father Vachon died, we are sure his love for the people of Cap de la Madeleine did not die nor did his love for Our Lady of the Cap; after all he had been with them forty-five years. Had he been praying? Well God sent the parish a priest; but just not another priest, one who would bring new life to the suffering souls of the Cap. The Curé of Ars said, *"If I had known when I arrived in Ars, all that I would have to suffer there, I would have died on the spot."*[4] In 1867, Father Désilets found 1000 hard-to-handle parishioners who knew little about the Faith and couldn't care less. No matter how hard he tried to reach them, the church remained basically empty on Sunday, with even fewer coming during the week, if that was possible.

Was God to allow this to continue? One night, Father was returning from hearing confessions in the vestry, when he stopped inside the church to pray. His heart almost broke! It was the eve of the Ascension and the church was empty! Then what should he see but a pig with a rosary dangling from his mouth! The thought came to him: *"The rosary falls from men's*

---

[3]from Bob and Penny Lord's chapter on St. John Vianney in their book: *"Saints and other Powerful Men in the Church."*
[4]from Bob and Penny Lord's chapter on St. John Vianney in their book: *"Saints and other Powerful Men in the Church."*

Above: *First Chapel in foreground and new Shrine of Our Lady of the Cap, Cap de la Madeleine, Canada*

Above: *Miraculous Statue of Our Lady of the Cap, Cap de la Madeleine, Canada*

Right: *Blessed Frederic witnessed the Miracle of the eyes of Our Lady of the Cap, Cap de la Madeleine, Canada*

hands to be picked up by the swine." What did he do? He wiped his tears, *"girded his loins,"*[5] put on the *"armor of God"*[6] and consecrated himself to Our Lady of the Rosary! He immediately began promoting devotion to the Rosary. At first, the reception was very cool, but little by little, more and more men, women and children flocked to the church to pray the Rosary. He restored the Brotherhood of the Rosary, which Father Vachon had founded 100 years before. The little church which had been empty, now could no longer hold the congregation. Talk began again, to build a new, larger church. [What can Our Lady do, if we only pray!]

Well the finances of the village were no better than they had been during Father Vachon's time; and the only stones they could use were on the other side of the St. Lawrence River. It did not look too hopeful; but nonetheless the building of the new church was approved and work began. On the other side of the St. Lawrence river, the stones were being split and prepared. All was in readiness for transport across the river for when winter set in; at that time they would be able to cart the stones over the river which would be frozen. There was only one problem; they were having a very balmy winter, with the temperatures never dropping even close to freezing. No ice - no transport! The parish did not have the resources to pay for the stones to be transported across the river by ferry - therefore no new church!

In November, Father Luc Désilets asked the people to pray that a bridge of ice form on the river, so that the building blocks could be carried across. Everyone began praying. The young associate pastor, Father Duquay, each day, prayed the Rosary at a side chapel, in front of the altar of the Brotherhood of the Most Holy Rosary, at the feet of Our Lady of the Cap.

March came and a high wind began to break up the ice blocking the mouth of the Saint-Maurice River to the south and

---

[5]Ex 12:11
[6]Eph 6:11

the north shore of the St. Lawrence River. The ice began to drift downstream to the Cap de la Madeleine. It was covering the river several hundred feet from the church. That Sunday, March 17th, Feast of St. Patrick, Father Duquay told the parishioners that there would be a High Mass for the feast of St. Joseph on March 19th, petitioning Jesus' foster father to ask his Son to form a bridge of ice! He also invited the men to come with him to survey the river. *(If they wanted it done immediately, they should have asked St. Patty! - An Irishman joking)*

When they arrived, they saw that where the river was covered with a thin layer of ice floating among drifts of snow. They went from spot to spot, looking for blocks of ice floating closely together. They had gone about 1000 feet with no success, when they spotted two of the guides heading upriver to the south shore. Father joined them. Only Father Duquay and the two guides dared continue, the ice was so thin and treacherous.

Having arrived at the south shore, Firmin Cadotte (one of the guides) crawled forward, feeling in the icy waters for a piece of ice that could carry his weight. He persisted and then was joined by thirty other men who began working alongside one another to form a 1600 foot stretch of ice along the river, wide enough for two carts carrying stones to pass one another. At 11 P.M., they returned to the sacristy and Father asked, *"Well men, what are we going to do now?"* A plan was formulated whereby they would pour water over the thin bridge of ice that had formed and, upon freezing, pour more water over it until it would become thicker, and when it was thick enough to carry the weight of the carts and stones, they would begin carting the stones across the river.

It was the following morning, March 18th, at 3 A.M., when the men returned to the river's edge and went back to work on the ice. Now considering how temperate it had been and that it was now March, it was nothing short of a miracle that the bridge was now solid enough to walk on! Men kept pouring water on the ice. It was now 6 inches thick! Encouraged, seeing a possible light at the end of the tunnel, they kept on pouring water.

March 19th, Feast of St. Joseph, just as they were trying to decide where the opening should be made for the carts to travel, as much snow had fallen during the night blocking the way, what did they see coming across the bridge of ice? The first cart carrying blocks of stone! This cart was followed by other carts, until by Sunday 175 sleighs carrying stones had passed. The men had carted 1000 feet of stone plus enough stone for a foundation. Father Duquay ordered all work to stop. God had answered their prayers; it was time to say *Thank You, Lord.* That day, the bridge was given the name it carries till today, *the Bridge of the Rosary.* One of the workers said, "*It was quite extraordinary, a real miracle. It defied common sense.*" And when Father Désilets saw what had come to pass, he said, "*Is this not a clear sign of Heavenly intervention? Can one not manifestly see the Finger of God?*"

On November 20, 1893, Father Duquay told his Bishop - Monsignor La Flèche:

"*...this is, to my mind, a great blessing from Almighty God, through Whom the Most Holy Virgin has chosen a plot of land in your modest diocese and has made it a center of Marian celebration...indeed I tell you, the Rosary which has been set up here will become a bulwark of our Faith.*"

A promise is made to the Blessed Virgin

Now, March of 1879, when the whole church was praying, another prayed and not only prayed, but made a promise to the Mother of God, that if She, at this advanced time of the season would grant him a bridge of ice strong enough for carriages to carry the stones needed for the church across the river, he, Father Désilets, would maintain the old church, and dedicate it in *perpetuity* as a place of devotion to our august Queen of Heaven, naming the church, "*Our Lady of the Most Holy Rosary.*"

The new church was built. It was filled, not only with

parishioners but the faithful from across the river; but times were still hard; too much to do, with too little money, and too little time to do it. Years flew by, finally ten years passed and still the old church had not been refurbished or dedicated. To give Father Désilets credit, all the parish's money had gone to build and maintain the new church; there were not enough resources to restore the old church. And to compound the problem, Father was called to spend more and more time with his Bishop in Rome clarifying problems that had risen in the diocese.

Father Désilets plan had been that when the old church was turned into a Shrine, there would be a spiritual director there to care for the Shrine, organize pilgrimages and be for the pilgrims who would be coming. Such a man would be Father Frederic!

Father Frederic comes to tend his Lady's Shrine

Blessed Frederic Jansoonne was born on the Flemish-Belgian border of France on November 19th, 1838. He was a traveling salesman for the cloth industry, from age sixteen through twenty-four, which we will see the Lord later use for His Glory. Frederic learned you cannot love two masters; you will love the one and hate the other.[7] Therefore as exciting and often challenging as his occupation could be, like Father Francis, the world and its allurements held no joy for him; Frederic joined the Franciscan Order in 1864. Five years later, friar Frederic was ordained a priest on August 17, 1870 at the age of thirty-one. He was soon sent to the Holy Land as a missionary and remained there for twelve years.

In the Holy Land, he was assigned to work as deputy-assistant to the keeper of holy places. Not satisfied with solely guiding pilgrims to the different Shrines dedicated to Jesus and Mary in Jerusalem and Galilee, Frederic worked towards bringing the pilgrims into a more intimate walk with Jesus and Mary. He renewed the tradition of processing through the streets

---

[7]Mt 6:24

of Jerusalem, following the Way of the Cross. He put new life
into pilgrimages coming to the Land of Jesus. His work there
would be a prelude to what God would ultimately call him to do
in Canada. The land where His Savior lived and died, would be
a training ground for the days to come. It would also help him in
the Shrine of Cap de la Madeleine when he built a Way of the
Cross there.

Frederic and Father Luc meet and Frederic is on his way.

Fr. Luc Désilets, pastor of the Church of Cap de la
Madeleine was in Rome on business with his Bishop. He had
been praying, concerned over the promise he had made to Mary
Most Holy; he had told Father Duquay that he *"most ardently
desired that Heaven should assure him that by dedicating the
tiny church to the honor of Mary, he was carrying out the wishes
of Our Lady and not indulging his own desires."*[8] Who should
he meet in Rome but a Franciscan named Father Frederic! He
believed that this was the sign Mother Mary was sending him
that it was truly She and not he who desired the Shrine. Father
Luc invited Father Frederic to come preach at his church in Cap
de la Madeleine. Father Frederic came and fell in love with the
area. Father Duquay later testified, at the Beatification
proceedings in 1927:

*"It was on "September 29, 1881, that I met the Servant of
God for the first time. He arrived from Trois-Rivières by
canoe...As I saw him coming up from the water's edge towards
Father Luc, who was waiting for him at the end of the
promontory, I was struck by his modest expression and
unassuming demeanor. Calm, spare of figure, austere, he
corresponded to my own image of St. Francis of Assisi."*

During his short time at Cap de la Madeleine, he made a
tremendous impression on Fr. Luc Désilets, who wrote:

*"You have sent us a Saint; both a Saint and a priest of
extraordinary power...He is universally sought after...The sick*

---

[8]quoting Father Duquay

*seek him out and follow him everywhere.   He is a man of
God...The more one has to do with him, the more one comes to
venerate and admire him...If you should see his superiors, you
may assure them that he lives like a Saint... You have to live
with this extraordinary man to really appreciate his virtue,
intelligence, warmheartedness and nobility."*

Sadly, Father Frederic was called back to the Holy Land in
May 1882. When he spoke of his departure, Father Frederic
said, *"I left Canada in May with regret in my heart, yet mingled
with some hope that I would return to that hospitable land, to
those simple folk living in the love of God..."*

The Lord was to answer his prayer.   Father Frederic
returned to Quebec on June 22, 1888. The old chapel had been
finally restored; it was only fitting Mother Mary would have her
son, the future custodian She had chosen, return the day it was to
be dedicated to Her.   There was a Holy Mass of Dedication, with
Father Luc as the celebrant and Father Frederic delivering the
homily, prophesying the future work of the Shrine:

*"Henceforth this Shrine shall be dedicated to Mary.
Pilgrims will come...from every family in the parish, from every
parish in the diocese in Canada. I tell you, that this modest
house of God will not suffice to hold the multitude of those who
will come to invoke the power and the munificence* (generosity)
of the gentle Virgin of the Most Holy Rosary."

Father Duquay said that Fr. Frederic *"was the moving
spirit of that unforgettable day."*

The Miracle of the Eyes

This was the day that the Lord chose to favor this Shrine
with a miracle! After the Mass, the statue of Our Lady du Cap
was taken from the side altar and placed above the tabernacle, on
the high altar, by this gesture conveying that from this day
forward, the church was no longer the parish church of Sainte
Marie de la Madeleine but, in thanksgiving for the Miracle of the
Bridge of the Rosary ten years before, it was now called the
Shrine of Notre Dame du Cap.

Father Frederic had been praying for a special sign from Our Lady all day. Now, evening was setting in, and it was time to close the church. There had been no sign. Nothing extraordinary had happened. Just at that moment, an invalid, Pierre LaCroix came to the two priests and asked if he could go into the church to pray to Our Lady. Father Frederic and Father Luc accompanied him into the church. They knelt down to pray, when the miracle took place. Father Frederic said:

"The statue of the Virgin had been sculpted with the eyes cast down. Now they were wide open, the gaze fixed. The Virgin was looking straight ahead, her eyes level. It could hardly be an optical illusion: her face was clearly visible, illuminated by the sun which, shining through one of the windows, filled the whole Shrine with light. Her eyes were black, well-shaped and in perfect harmony with the rest of her face. The Virgin's expression was that of a living person, at once grave and sad. This marvel lasted somewhere between five and ten minutes."

Father Frederic would never be the same! His Lady had answered him!

The handicapped man, Pierre Lacroix, made this statement:

"I went into the Shrine about seven o'clock in the evening. I was with Father Luc Désilets and Father Frederic...Well, I was praying and then I took a look at the Holy Virgin, just in front of me. I could see clearly that the statue's eyes were wide open. She looked quite natural, just as if she was staring over our heads.

"I didn't say a word, just went on looking at the statue, when Father Désilets got up - he was on my right - and went over to Father Frederic and I heard him say: `Do you see it?' `Yes' Father Frederic answered, `the statue has opened its eyes, hasn't it.' `Yes it has. But is this really taking place?'

"So I said that I'd seen the same thing, been watching it for several minutes, and I'm making this solemn declaration

because I believe in my heart and conscience that it is true and I know that this declaration has the same force and binding effect as if it had been made under oath."

Those who saw *"the miracle of the eyes,"* saw it as a sign from Heaven expressing the wish that pilgrims be drawn to this Shrine. The news spread like a forest fire; pilgrims converged on the Shrine; that same year 1500 pilgrims came to the Shrine on June 24th, a national holiday. By the end of the year, 10,000 pilgrims had come to venerate Mary Most Holy at her Shrine at Cap de la Madeleine.

A few weeks later, a jubilant Father Luc said, *"This our undertaking is desired by God and required of the Holy Virgin."* Two months after the consecration, Father would go to where the Lord and His Mother could personally thank him; Father Luc died, suddenly, without warning; he was only fifty-six years old. He died peacefully; but before he died, he turned confidently to Father Duquay and said, *"Father Frederic will help you. It is no accident of Providence that he is here with us."*

August 30, 1888, the Bishop of the diocese assigned the vocation of pastor to Father Duquay, and at the same time asked Father Frederic to assist Father Duquay with the finances of the parish and the task of welcoming pilgrims to the Shrine. Father Frederic worked alongside Father Duquay for fourteen years, until the Oblates of Mary took over the Shrine, in 1902. In addition, Father Frederic established a Center for the Holy Land in Trois-Rivières. Father Frederic was the first Spiritual Director of Pilgrimages coming to the Shrine of Notre Dame du Cap. Father Duquay said that although he was the pastor, Father Frederic was the *"moving spirit which animated the work."*

Father Frederic was a remarkable spirit-filled homilist and a prolific writer. He spread devotion to the Way of the Cross. He founded Third Order Franciscan chapters, everywhere he traveled in Quebec. He wrote many books and pamphlets, carrying them in a satchel, bringing them with him, distributing them wherever he went. He would sell books and magazines when he gave talks, or to anyone he met, giving all the money to the Shrine to help finance the building of Notre-Dame du Cap. He built a Way of the Cross, fashioned after the one in Jerusalem. It has since been replaced by a new one, built after his death.

People began calling him a Saint during his lifetime, as he was well-known for his sanctity and virtuous life. At his Golden Jubilee in 1915, at the dinner celebrating his fifty years as a Franciscan, Fr. Duquay told Fr, Frederic that their achievement[9] was his alone, since nothing had been *achieved* without him.

Our Saint goes Home - Our Lord and His Mother welcoming him - Job well done, son of Francis!

On the 25th of August, 1916, Father Frederic died in Montreal. His body reposes till today, in the Franciscan church located on 890 St. Maurice in Trois-Rivières, in the province of Quebec.

At his funeral, the Bishop of Trois-Rivières, eulogized him in the following way:

"It was Father Frederic who played the major role in the devotional undertaking of Our Lady of the Rosary in Cap de la Madeleine. The man known, justifiably, as the `prophet of Notre-Dame du Cap,' carried out an immense task during the fourteen years he worked as director of pilgrimages. Like the Saints, he rendered all glory and all praise to God."

At the Cause for the Beatification of Father Frederic in 1927, Father Duquay stated:

"I knew Father Frederic over a period of thirty-five years...He was my mentor, my support, my guiding angel in the various undertakings of my sacerdotal career. When, as an assistant priest and later parish priest, I faced financial difficulties, dealing with organized pilgrimages, he was providential and helped me to control both the spiritual and temporal aspects of my task with skill and kindness.

---

[9]attributing the building of the shrine at Cap de la Madeleine to him

"I do believe he died like a Saint...He never claimed to have wrought miracles...He had a childlike trust in the Holy Virgin...He used to speak of her with tears in his eyes. There came a time when his devotion to the Most Holy Virgin took over his whole life and he became an artisan of an estimable and admirable piece of work. I am referring to, of course, the pilgrimages to Cap de la Madeleine...

"Thanks to him, the word spread of this Shrine that Mary had chosen and marked out with her preference...The Shrine soon became the meeting ground for every kind of physical and moral distress. The sick found healing, the sinners were filled with deep remorse and penitence."

Pope John Paul II came as a pilgrim to Cap de la Madeleine on September 10th, 1984, and then on the 25th of September, 1988, he beatified Frederic, the holy priest who was instrumental in spreading the message of the Shrine to our Lady, which today and for many centuries has been so well known and revered by not only the people of Quebec, but from the other provinces of Canada, the United States, Haiti, the West Indies, Latin America, and throughout Europe.

As is the case with another apparition of our Lady in Pontmain, France, Our Lady of Cap de la Madeleine offers and assures all who come of her loving intercession. As many attest, her Son has listened and many miracles have been documented attesting to her ongoing intervention.

Men dared to dreamed the impossible, and God did the miraculous. In each century, in each country, God has a Blessed Frederic in mind; all you have to do is say Yes!

Blessed Junípero Serra
Apostle of California

Much maligned, and most misunderstood at this time, is the Saint we dare to write of, Junípero Serra! When we live in a topsy-turvy world where to talk of God is not *"politically correct,"* it is no wonder that the *father of lies* would dare spread all sorts of lies, in an effort to kill the memory of a true Role Model and demean the work he did. The enemy of God has always done everything possible, to slander and render useless anyone who would remind us of the reason we were born, to love God, to know Him and to serve Him.

Daring to take the serpent on, our life is dedicated to speaking of those who courageously served the Lord, withstanding the slings and the arrows of their time. Our story is about a man from Mallorca, a sleepy, breathtakingly beautiful island off the coast of Spain, a man filled with love and peace, a missionary who *reluctantly* answered the call to evangelize!

Our story is not only about a Saint but about a land blessed by the blood of martyrs, its every mile named after the holy - *Sacramento* (after the Blessed Sacrament), *San Francisco* (St. Francis), *San José* (St. Joseph), *Santa Ana* (St. Ann, Mary's mother), *San Gabriel* (St. Gabriel the Archangel), *Los Angeles* (after Our Lady Queen of the Angels of the Portiuncola[1]), *Santa Clara* (St. Clare), *Santa Monica* (St. Monica), *San Antonio* (St. Anthony), to mention just a few of the thousands of places blessed by the missionaries who gave their lives to come to this land and bring the Word of God. Our story is a call to the people of the United States to remember those who came before us, and take back our country from the false gods set up by the enemy of God, and once again consecrate our fair land to the true God, Our Founder and Mary Our Queen!

History is history, and sometimes history can be offensive to certain peoples, but it does not make history less history;

---

[1]St. Francis' first little church, located in Assisi

Left: ***Blessed Junípero Serra
Apostle of California
Founder of the many
Missions that dot the coast
of California from San
Diego to San Francisco***

Right: ***Blessed Junípero
Serra was baptized at San
Pedro Parish Church***

Left: ***Blessed Junípero Serra spent
eighteen years of his life at the
Convento San Francisco in
Palma, Mallorca.
Interior of the Church of San
Francisco adjoining the Convento***

whereas to sometimes accommodate certain cultures, we sacrifice the truth by taking away all that came to pass to form us into the people we are, today. Our story is about Junípero Serra, a true missionary of God!

In a time when the Name of God is not to be mentioned in schools, a time when children no longer say the Pledge of Allegiance to the United States, because the Name of God is referred to, and it would offend those few who do not believe in God, it is important that we set the record straight about a Saint who brought God to this nation, this nation, which we have forgotten was founded under God.

I remember once thinking how wise was the publisher who put on his newspaper the standard, *"The truth will make you free."* Well I do not know what truth he was referring to; I only know Jesus is the **Truth**, the Way and the Life; the only Truth, Way and Life. As the Truth Who is God is being taken away from us, inch by inch, truth has become what the media tells us is truth, people who write under the guise of being *objective* writing very *subjectively*. And we allow them to influence our lives and the future of our children!

Well, we are not here to be *"politically correct,"* to compromise Our Lord Who is the Truth to win a popularity contest; we are about the business of saving souls, our own, yours, and the souls of our families. Read on about a Saint who came with thirty-two other missionaries to this continent, the reluctant Apostle of California - Junípero Serra. If you, like we, wish to reclaim California and the United States, for that matter the world, for Our Lord, His Mother, the Angels and the Saints, then read on and pass on the story of our *reluctant missionary*, the one whom Pope John Paul II (who also dares to be *"politically incorrect"* for the Kingdom), raised to the Annals of the Blesseds, and is on his way toward raising him to the Halls of the Saints.

Call to Sainthood!

Why does God take one child and leave another? No one knows the answer; only when we are standing before the Throne of God will we know and then it won't matter. Our story begins in the little town of Petra in Mallorca. It's November 24, 1713; suddenly a baby's cry rings out and an announcement is made: A boy is born! No sooner did Junípero Serra let out his first sound, his godparents immediately brought him to the church to be baptized, as a precaution, because his two siblings before him had died soon after birth, without having received the Sacrament which cleanses us of Original Sin.

"I baptize you Miguel, in the Name of the Father, and the Son and the Holy Spirit." With those words having been intoned, the baby Miguel anointed, the young member, just hours old, was on his way to serve Mother Church. As he would need his Heavenly Mother who would be with him wherever he ventured, as with the custom with all the people of Mallorca, weeks later, his mother and father brought their son to the Shrine on the side of the hill, to their *Nuestra Señora de Bon Any*[2] (Our Lady of the Good Year). As she was the Patron of Petra, the islanders would climb 1000 feet up the mountain to petition Our Lady for a good crop (for example), then return and give her thanks for their prayers having been answered; and as in this case, entrusting Her with their most precious treasure, their baby, introducing Jesus' Mother and theirs, to their new-born and She to the child as his (or her) Mother.

Months later, when the baby Miguel began to take his first steps, his parents brought him to *Nuestra Señora de los Angeles* (Our Lady of the Angels),[3] where they would consecrate their child to Our Lady and her Angels, and from that day forward be protected under the Mantle of Mother Mary. He was confirmed two years later in 1715. He always felt the calling to the

---

[2] in the dialect of the island which is closer to Catalan than Spanish
[3] as is the custom in Mallorca

religious life. His biography states that he was so in love with St. Francis and his followers, he wanted to wear the Franciscan habit while still a child, but he had to wait.

The Serras were farmers, the whole family, several generations - grandparents, parents, their children, each morning all went off to work in the fields. It was back-breaking work which began when the sun began to peek into the dusk of dawn and ended as the sun mercifully set to let the quiet of night and rest take over. No sooner was dinner over, too tired to even speak, they all dropped off to a much needed sleep.

Miguel (Junípero) came from not only a family of strong Catholics, whose lives revolved around church, but a people who for generations had remained faithful to the Church, through centuries of invasions from Saracens and Moors, fighting for and preserving their most treasured possession - the Catholic Faith.

Now, as with the other youngsters, Miguel could not be spared to receive an education. He was needed in the fields. For that matter, how much book learning was necessary to do the grueling work which needed only a strong back supported by an equally strong will. But when God has a plan... Every spare moment, when he was not needed to help with the chores, Miguel could be found listening to the friars at the Franciscan Church and the Convent of San Bernardino, which by God's design was just a few hundred yards from his home. Miguel was fascinated by the stories of Francis' life, and always pressed the friars to read to him from *The Little Flowers of St. Francis*. As fascinated as Miguel was with the life Francis adopted, from *"spoiled rich boy"* to *"poor one"* (living a voluntary life with Lady Poverty), he was most drawn to the life that Francis' followers *continued* to live. This, their true living out of their founder's Rule, was what most deeply called him to the religious life. The Franciscans, on their part, were touched by the eagerness he had to learn; he was like a sponge soaking up every drop of lifegiving knowledge of Church. After he quickly learned how to read and write, the friars graduated him to mastering Latin.

When this came to his parent's attention, they relieved him more and more from his chores, to pursue his studies. Pleased and amazed by the progress Miguel was making, his parents sent him off to study with a priest in Palma, a larger city; he was fifteen at the time. Soon Miguel recognized his walk was as a Franciscan friar and after being rejected because of his youth and small size (he was barely 5'2"),[4] he was finally accepted and began his journey. He had to be granted special permission by his instructors, to begin his novitiate. In 1730, just short of his seventeenth birthday, his joy was complete - he donned the habit of St. Francis. After one year of intense studies, he took his vows of poverty, chastity and obedience on September 15th, 1731, becoming a full-fledged friar, to be known from that day on by the name of Francis' companion, the *"Jester of God"*[5] - *Fray Junípero Serra.*

He delved into his studies, his eyes and heart on becoming a priest and professor. He took three years of philosophy, then followed by digging into theology and the many subjects required to attain his final goal. Junípero was ordained subdeacon on December 18, 1734, then deacon a year and a half later. He was ready; he had completed his studies with flying colors; but because he was less than the required age of twenty-four, he could not be ordained to the Priesthood. At this time, he adopted a motto from St. Paul which would become his vanguard in his missionary work: *"Always go forward, never turn back."*

As there were no restrictions regarding teaching, after months of grueling preparation, he was tested and accepted unanimously as professor of philosophy. He was brilliant, and if you would have asked anyone what his vocation was, they would have replied emphatically - as a brilliant teacher, imparting his superior intellect and wisdom. He was regarded highly by everyone, especially two students who would become part of his

[4]I cannot see their problem; St. Francis was not quite that height.
[5]as he was called

endeavor in the New World - Francisco Palóu and Juan Crespi.

He was ordained between 1737 and 1739, the exact date is not known. He continued studying and received his Doctorate in Theology. After that he became a professor of Theology at the Pontifical, Imperial, Royal and Literary University of Mallorca. He continued in this capacity until he was thirty-five years old, in 1748.

He became looked upon as one of the greatest homilists and orators of Mallorca. He was awarded the honor of preaching in the Cathedral on the Feast of Corpus Christi, a privilege bestowed upon only the most renowned orators. He continued to deliver impassioned sermons for the next six years to the people of Mallorca, imploring them to have hope, offering them much needed encouragement, as they struggled to come out from under the horrendous drought and plague that had devastated them and their land.

He was asked to deliver the sermon on the Feast Day of Ramon Llull, the university's Patron Saint. Now, this was possibly the dream of every homilist, but suddenly it was hollow; Junípero found no joy in the accolades he had been receiving; his accomplishments no longer satisfied him; there was an emptiness inside him which longed to be filled. Junípero had read the lives of the Saints and had dreamed to follow in their footsteps, especially those of his Seraphic Father Francis. But when the opportunity came for him to go to evangelize the Indians in the New World, he hemmed and hawed; after all his new charges would not be able to benefit from all his years of study and hard work to become a theologian and orator; did God want him to waste that?

When Mezquía had first offered him a place on the mission, he had refused; then when he decided to go, there were no openings. Junípero took that as a sign from the Lord that He wanted him to remain where he was. But then Mezquía notified him there *were* openings. The five men, who had volunteered to go, after seeing the wild waves beating against the shore, took it as a foreshadowing of the hazardous voyage ahead, grew frightened and backed out.   Junípero knew it was God summoning him to go. As we can see, Serra was leaving glory and acceptance, behind; he didn't have to go to the New World to make his name in the world. So when the foolish attack Junípero Serra, they need consider they may be attacking God Himself Who chose him.

Junípero stood up to deliver his homily; suddenly all the thirst Junípero had to be a missionary, a martyr, an evangelist for Christ, burst forth.   No more doubts; no more leaving to tomorrow.   Because of his many studies, and his desire to become a Doctor of Theology, he had put his dreams on the back burner. Now, he believed that the Lord was sending him to fulfill the role He had fashioned for him, from before he was born. When he delivered his homily, all the pent-up passion he had stored away, to walk in the footsteps of the martyrs before him, came forth and he was on his way to the New World. All those who listened were grieved because they knew they would never see their beloved Junípero again.   There is nothing recorded of that sermon, only that which one of his fellow professors said: *"This sermon is worthy of being printed in letters of gold."*

Junípero and Francisco Palóu sail for Mexico

It took four months for the ship to be made ready to cross the treacherous Atlantic.   Unlike those who had stayed behind out of fear of drowning at sea, Junípero's misgivings and struggles were between his love for family and God. He wrote to Francisco, a fellow priest at the university to pass this message on to his parents:

"Tell them that words cannot express the feelings of my heart as I bid them farewell.   Please be a consolation to my parents to sustain them in their sorrow.   I wish I could communicate to them the great joy that fills my heart. If I could do this, then surely they would encourage me to go forward and never turn back.   Let them remember that the office of an apostolic preacher (missionary), especially in its actual

exercise, is the greatest calling to which they could wish me to be chosen."

He then told Francisco to remind his parents that it was their faith and devotion that first filled him with his love of God. His words to his parents read something like this:

"I shall never get over the loss of not being able to be near you, but the most important thing I have to do is the Will of God. It is for the love of God that I leave you, and only with His Grace that I have the strength to do so. Rejoice that you have a son who is a priest, though an unworthy one and a sinner, who daily in the Holy Sacrifice of the Mass prays for you, that the Lord sustain you, give you your daily bread, patience in your trials and resignation to His Holy Will, courage to fight the evil one, and last of all when it is God's Will a happy and tranquil death in His holy Grace. If I succeed in becoming a good religious, my prayers will be more powerful and you will benefit from them."

It reminds me of what St. Teresa of Avila wrote:

"Upon leaving my father's house, I knew I would not, even at the very moment and agony of my death, feel the anguish of separation more painfully than at that point in time." She went on to say, *"not even the love of God I had inside me could make up for the love I felt for my father and friends."*[6]

On April 13, 1749, Junípero Serra and Francisco Palóu sailed for Mexico, his first leg in a lifetime journey. He would never see his parents again.

His travels from Mallorca to Mexico took him from April 13, 1749 to December 7, 1749, one week short of eight months. The ocean was so rough, most of the missionaries became deadly ill, including Francisco Palóu; they were so sick they were afraid they would die before they landed; all that is but Junípero Serra who, although he battled fevers and bouts of nausea like the

---

[6]from St. Teresa of Avila, a chapter in Bob and Penny Lord's book: *Saints and other Powerful Women in the Church.*

others, was able to sustain himself through the long arduous voyage - with little or no water, and barely enough to eat to feed a baby.   Throughout it all, Junípero prayed and encouraged everyone to go on!   On the way they stopped in Puerto Rico where, during their 18 day stop-over, they celebrated Holy Mass, heard confessions round the clock, and generally administered the Sacraments.

At last Mexico!

The ship set foot on Mexican soil the day before the Feast of the Immaculate Conception of Our Lady.   They landed in Veracruz, two hundred miles from Mexico City.   Although the King of Spain had provided horses to transport them, Junípero, true Friar that he was, chose to walk, as those other great missionaries to the New World before him.   It sounds so glamorous, when we hear they walked along the *Camino Real*! In actuality it was a poor, dirt road, unsafe because of frequent attacks by warring tribes, bandits, and wild animals; and if none of these finished you off, there was always the threat of avalanches - rocks cascading down upon you, killing you.   It is said that Serra and his solitary companion - another Franciscan, arrived in Mexico City, eighteen days later.   They traveled over mountains, with no provisions, depending on what food or shelter they could beg from people inhabiting the areas they passed. Many nights they slept out in the open, Junípero clutching his crucifix to his chest, often awakening the next morning, half frozen.

A stranger comes to their aid

Serra later spoke of an unexplainable incident, on his journey to Mexico City: Evening was fast approaching, when Junípero and his companion stood at the edge of an ominous looking, dangerous, highly turbulent river.   It was obvious they were lost and the river unsafe to cross.   Junípero cried out for help, when suddenly a well-dressed man seemed to appear from out of nowhere.   He pointed to a shallow section in the river where they could cross. When they arrived on the other side, the man was waiting for them; he gave them shelter for the night, but when they tried to engage him in conversation, he remained quiet, going about his way serving them. When they rose the following morning, they awakened to the ground covered with ice; they would have frozen to death, had they not been helped by the generous stranger.

They had traveled quite a distance, when they paused to rest. The last few days had been hard; they were suffering from exhaustion; they were near-starved; what little food they had was gone, and they had not eaten in days. Then a figure on horseback approached them. He had been traveling in the opposite direction. He turned his horse toward them, galloped over and bent down; he handed each of them a pomegranate; then rode off leaving them to shake their heads, conjecturing on how much the rider looked like the man who had given them shelter days ago.

Farther down the road, a farmer gave the two a place in his barn to spend the night. When they rose the next morning, they celebrated Mass and the farmer gave them a loaf of bread for the journey. Saving the loaf for later, who should they encounter but a beggar. They gave the poor starving man the bread. The night found the two by the roadside, tired and hungry. Again, the rider who had given them the pomegranate rode up to them. He reached into his saddlebag and pulled out a small, lumpy, unappetizing loaf of bread. He took his knife and cut it in two, handing each of them half. The bread emitted such a foul smell, they were sure it was spoiled, and would make them sick; although reticent to eat it, their hunger took over and they devoured it. It was delicious and filling! The stranger now out of sight, Junípero came to the conclusion that the mysterious stranger was not a stranger at all; but the foster father of Jesus, St. Joseph who not mysteriously, but *miraculously* came to their rescue.

Above: ***Father Serra landed at Monterey California, June 3, 1770***

Below:
***The cell of Father Serra at Mission
San Carlos Borromeo de Carmelo***

Right: ***Statue of Father Serra at Mission
San Juan Capistrano***

Junípero arrives in Mexico City and the preparations begin.
The missionaries were required to spend a year preparing
for evangelizing to the Indians in the wild. As only God would
be able to bring about the conversion of the natives to His Heart,
they spent time in cloister, first praying, then getting ready
physically and mentally to face a brand new civilization totally
foreign to them. They studied the various tongues of the tribes to
whom they would minister; they received insights from other
missionaries already preaching in Mexico; and then using the
implements that were indigenous to the area and the people they
were trying to reach, they learned how to farm this new land.

Serra proved himself a brilliant student, quickly absorbing
all there was to learn. Once he began giving sermons, they soon
discovered what an outstanding homilist he was, and they did not
want to let him go. They petitioned the Guardian Franciscan to
keep Serra there in Mexico City, arguing his knowledge of
Theology was of great importance, and more beneficial to the
faithful who understood; surely it would be wasted on the simple,
uneducated Indians. Of course, Junípero Serra would hear
nothing of it and insisted he be on his way.

They needed volunteers to go to Sierra Gorda, and
although their year was not up, Junípero joined seven other
missionaries and they were on their way to evangelize to the
most unbending opponents of the Spanish settlers, the Pame
Indians. The Pames waylaid and attacked soldiers relentlessly,
as they resisted all attempts at coexisting. The task of trying to
bring the God of the Spaniards to them would be no small task
for the new missionaries. Spanish conquistadors had defeated
the Pames Indians in battle, but had not won their hearts, so the
victory was short-lived.

Whereas one of the missionaries, Fr. Mezquía, in 1740,
got them to listen. He told them he proposed sending
missionaries who would befriend them. The Pames were so
touched by the love and compassion shown them by the
Franciscans, seven thousand converted and came into the

missions. They lived together, Indians and Spaniards, learning from one another, until a disease foreign to the Indians, an epidemic of Small-Pox wiped out two thirds of the Pames living in the missions. Four missionary priests died from the disease and the rest left, thoroughly discouraged!

What Serra and the other missionaries were told was that they would find 1000 Indian converts in the mission. This was greatly exaggerated! The Spanish soldiers had abused them, uprooted them from their tribes; Serra met few Indians and those few were starving; he found that those inside the mission were Indians working for the soldiers at the fort, rather than Christians. Serra was determined to change all that!

Father Serra began implementing the things that made it work under Fr. Mezquía. When the sun rose, the mission bells would sound, calling all the natives to church. Attendance was required of all who lived within the mission walls. Each day either Father Serra or Father Palóu[7] recited the daily prayers and read from the Bible, in Latin; and then they translated it into the Pame language, teaching the Indians what it meant to those of Jesus' time and meant to those living in *their* time. Catechism classes on the Faith and its place in their lives were given twice a day, to all children starting from as young as five years old.

As is the teaching of the Church, all converts or catechumens were required to attend Mass on Sunday, on Holy Days of Obligation and at all funeral Masses. When Mass was over, all the parishioners, Spaniards and Indians, alike, filed past the priest and kissed his hand.[8] Missionaries would visit those

---

[7]Both studied the Pame language

[8]As the priest is *"in persona Christi"* and during the Mass, his hands bring us Jesus, in His Body, Blood, Soul and Divinity, then it is only fitting we pay respect to him and his consecrated hands. This practice was always followed around the world until changes came about as a result of confusion resulting from a misunderstanding of the documents of Vatican Council II. In Mexico and Europe, there are still parishes that practice this reverent display, today.

who had missed Mass and try to convince them to return to church and reject their pagan practices. They patiently went about instructing them how much Jesus - the One True God loved them, how He had died once and for all, His death and sacrifice appeasing God the Father, Who from that time on no longer required human sacrifice, and does not require it from them.

The missionaries did not try to evangelize by disparaging the Indian's false gods, but tried to change their hearts by teaching them about the unconditional love the One True God had for all His children, no matter what race, color or creed, including them and the Spanish settlers. In this way, the Indians began recognizing the difference between their gods and the God of the Christians and many converted! We call that loving persuasion. And it worked, far better than the foolish, senseless tactics of intimidation by soldiers who instead used force, to the horror of Serra and the other missionaries who openly condemned this.

There were laws set up by the Spanish soldiers, one of which was the outlawing of all pagan rituals. But the missionaries knew that was not the way; you cannot destroy someone's belief, as everyone needs to believe in something or Someone; they knew what they had to do was build a bridge for the natives to walk over. Cachum, whom the Indians revered as the *mother of the sun*, was the answer! On top of the mountain Sierra Gorda, there was a temple built to Cachum, with a handsomely carved statue of her within, where the Indians would come and ask for favors, do atonement (usually by sacrifice) and leave gifts of grain and sacrificed animals on her altar.

What Father Serra saw was reminiscent of the steps which the natives of Petra took to the Shrine of *Nuestra Señora de Bon Any.* The Indians, too, climbed to the top of their mountain, only up a staircase[9] carved out of the mountain, where, instead of a Catholic Shrine and Our Lady of the Good Year, the Temple and

---

[9]along which the Indians buried their chiefs and other prominent figures

the *mother of the sun* were awaiting them. The Indians and the Christians from Spain had *more* than *less* in common, only not knowing one another, never discovering their kindred spirits, they had their differences separate and kill them.

How to bring them together? They both loved pomp and pageantry! Father Serra knew what to do! He would place a huge Cross on top of the mountain and build fourteen graphic Stations of the Cross,[10] leading to the top of the mountain, each station with figures recreating the events along the Way of the Cross which led to the Passion and Death of Our Lord Jesus Christ. Father Serra ordered the Stations of the Cross to be constructed in such a way, leading up the mountain, they reminded the Indians of the staircase to the *mother of the sun*, and a link was made in the bond that would hold them together as a family, some day.

Good Friday, 1751, the Indians watched as the first Stations of the Cross were made with Father Serra carrying the Cross up the mountain on his shoulders, re-enacting the Lord's horrific Way of the Cross. At the top, Father placed a carved wooden statue of Christ and nailed it to the Cross. Then the Christus was removed from the Cross and placed in a wooden coffin. Up to this time, they had *heard* the words; now they were *witnessing* the price the One True God paid; they understood and they wept. Easter Sunday, the wooden figure of Christ was taken from the coffin, dressed in fine robes and processed around the mission; the Scandal of the Cross was now the Triumph of the Cross and the end of all sacrifice.

They understood! No more worshipping the *mother of the sun*; they had learned how the One True God had left *His Mother* to them. Now, each Sunday evening, after the sun went down, a beautiful statue of Our Lady was carried throughout the mission on a litter, by Indian braves who competed for this honor. She

---

[10]The practice of making the Stations of the Cross was a relatively new devotion, which the Pope allowed only the Franciscans to observe.

was accompanied by lit torches mystically lighting the way.

Feast Days were celebrated with the same kind of awe and majesty, the pageant beginning after the Indians had heard the life of the Saint being honored; it was the ancient concept of the morality plays with which the early Church taught.

Word spread and began attracting Indians from surrounding tribes and Spaniards as well, enemies now brothers in the One True God Who made them family! Franciscan missionaries began building churches in their missions and the Faith grew, and with it the peace that the Spaniards could not bring about through force and bribery.

All who met him were amazed at his endless energy. Never too tired, too discouraged to get up another day and serve, he celebrated daily Mass, instructed the catechumens and continued to educate Indians who had converted to the Faith, as well as the Spanish settlers. He worked on designing and building the different churches in the missions of the Sierra Gorda. He personally visited the sick, making sure they were well cared for in the mission infirmary. He tirelessly administered the Sacraments, no matter the distance, the weather or the present danger. But with all that, he never neglected his daily prayers. Last of all, ever faithful to church authority, he kept the Apostolic College of San Fernando in Mexico City abreast of all that was transpiring in the missions - always ready to obey their command.

He was obedient, above all! After having served the Pame Indians at Jalpan[11] for nine years, September 1758, it looked as if he was about to leave and go on to missions farther up north. Two missionaries had been killed in Texas and they needed Serra and Palóu to take their place. He was exhilarated, at first! Then he looked around nostalgically at what God and man's faith in Him had accomplished the nine years he was blessed to be there. When he first arrived, all there was, were tiny crudely built

---

[11]it is in the state of Querétaro

Above: *Pope John Paul II visits the tomb of Blessed Junípero Serra September 1987 at Mission San Carlos Borromeo del Carmelo*

Above: *Mission San Carlos Borromeo del Carmelo founded by Blessed Junípero Serra*

Above: *Blessed Junípero Serra's beatification ceremony Sept. 25, 1988*

adobes, barely protected from the elements by thatched roofs and a few Indians at the foot of an 11,000 foot mountain. Now there was a thriving mission filled with educated, devoted members of the Pame tribe who had accepted the Church as their own, living peacefully side-by-side with their Spanish neighbors. He would miss them; but, never looking back, he was filled with excitement at what lay ahead.

Father Serra and Father Palóu leave for Mexico City.

Fathers Serra and Palóu leave for Mexico City and their next assignment. Only their next assignment was not to be Texas. It seems a difference developed about who would run the mission and who would be the new custodians. The Apostolic College chose Serra and Palóu, but the Spaniard who was the original benefactor insisted on choosing the new missionaries; so, they agreed to disagree and that mission was never reopened.

Serra did not return to his beloved Sierra Gorda, but was to remain in Mexico City, serving as choir master and novice master, for the next nine years! A light cannot be hidden under a bushel basket. His fame as an intellectual and astute Spiritual Director reached the ears of the Spanish gentry and he was in great demand. Although this would have been an opportune time to ingratiate himself with the finest families of Mexico City, who could help him financially in the future, he never visited their homes. If they wished his counsel, they had to come to the College.

He went into the surrounding areas of Mexico City preaching, like John the Baptist before him, of the need to repent! His spirituality had grown to more fasting, mortification, penance and sacrifice. He often shared with Palóu, he had no desire but to revive the feelings he had in his novitiate when he learned of the Saints.

Out of death, comes life.

Life is not always fair. We have just finished writing about St. Ignatius of Loyola and his Company of Jesus, than we find them under attack! Their apostolate and missionary work grew, until it reached the far corners of every continent except Australia. Rapid success brings about lack of communication and often misunderstanding, and sometimes jealousy. The Jesuits were interfering with the greed which pervaded the times; and tried to block the kings from exploiting the colonies. They were proving a threat to all the royal houses who feared they were trying to form states of their own. In 1758, there was a pact between the Bourbon courts of France, Spain, Naples and Parma to get rid of the Jesuits.

Charles III remained friendly to the Jesuits, but his ministers were always against them. After the death of the Queen Mother, the King became under the full influence of his ministers. The Queen now out of the way, they began their plot to get rid of the Jesuits. They produced a forged letter allegedly written by the Superior General of the Jesuits charging that Charles was not the legitimate heir to the throne and that at the proper time he would produce proof. As this would threaten his claim to the throne, without thoroughly investigating, King Charles III called a special session of the *Extraordinary Council* on January 29th, 1767; the Jesuits were declared *instigators of rebellion* and by a royal decree, were banished from Spain and her colonies.

Now, the Jesuits had made enemies in the New World; they had objected to the ill treatment suffered by the Indians at the hands of certain Spanish settlers and soldiers. Therefore, it was with great delight, on the morning of June 25th, 1767, that soldiers encircled all twenty-nine Jesuit missions and churches in Mexico, and rousing the surprised Jesuits from their sleep, read the King's orders they be expelled and all their property, along with the missions be seized! The priests had time to take only their prayer books and the clothes on their backs. They were jailed like common criminals and thrown into the hold of a ship going to Veracruz. So enraged and frightened was the King, he quite madly decreed: *"If after the embarkation there should be found one Jesuit in the district, even if ill or dying, the government officials responsible, would suffer the penalty of death.*" The very few who lived through that horrible voyage, arrived back in Spain to face charges.

The long dusty, desolate road to California!

A little older, he is now fifty-four years old, his hair is a little grayer, and Father Serra is summoned to appear at the Apostolic College in Mexico City to be apprised of a new assignment - he is to be the new president of missions formerly run by the Society of Jesus, in Baja California. Now Baja, by no stretch of the imagination would be considered a plum of an assignment! This stretch of narrow land surrounded by nothing but water, its air and land made desolate by its unyielding aridity, earned it the fond title *"the last corner on earth."* The missions had been placed in the custody of the Franciscans by the King of Spain, Charles III, and all Father Serra could do was obey!

When Serra arrived at his new post, the 40,000 Indians reported by the Jesuits were now a mere 8,000. Serra, who loved the Indians dearly, described them as a handsome people. But sadly, the huts were so poor and conditions so deplorable, 1000 Indians were dying each year, and the death rate of infants 100%. It is believed that Indian women were purposely aborting their babies rather than have them starve to death. Disease finished off those Indians who did not die of starvation. Father Palóu prophesied, if conditions remained as they were, Baja would be left without a single soul. Father Serra's year here, which had begun with so much enthusiasm, ended with disappointment. At first, not in keeping with the other missions in Mexico, the missionaries were to have a say in only the spiritual aspects of the missions. When the newly appointed inspector general saw the impossible conditions, he most willingly handed over all the responsibility to Father Serra and the missionaries. No sooner did Serra begin to work on change, than he was summoned to engage in the evangelization of what was called then *Alta California* (or California).

In 1542, an explorer in the service of the Crown of Spain, while serving with Cortes, claimed the coast of California from San Diego to Monterey for Spain. Then another Spaniard came in 1579, and he laid claim to Alta California in the name of Spain. In 1579, Sir Francis Drake claimed San Francisco for England.

For a least 100 years, lacking the resources, Spain did nothing about her claim. Then in 1760, the Crown of Spain could feel Russia's hot breath on their necks, ready to strike. The threatening Bear from the East[12] began blazing a trail, along the Northwest coastline of the New World, first colonizing Alaska, and then advancing ominously southward, with the rapid establishment of settlements extending to Point Reyes.[13] Now as Point Reyes is just north of San Francisco and Britain was showing a sudden renewed interest in San Francisco, Spain could see two colonizing rivals closing in on her and her possessions to the south (Mexico - then called New Spain). The Crown decided to act. Still no better off financially, Spain enlisted the aid of the Franciscan missionaries to settle Alta California.

In 1769, when Friar Junipero had been transferred to Baja or lower California, although *man* thought it was for him to run the fifteen missions seized from the Jesuits, God had another idea. Father Serra was informed, barely one year after having arrived in Baja that he was to pioneer the settlement of missions in Alta or upper California.

On July 1, 1769, he arrived in San Diego, and on July 2nd, he celebrated the first Mass in what is now known as the famous California Missions. He was 56 and the biggest challenge of his life faced him, all that he had received in education, all the spiritual preparations he had made, the austerities he had practiced most of his life would be for this one act, this his last gift to the Lord and His Mother. California would be

---

[12]Russia
[13]Marin county, California

consecrated, every hill, valley, mountain, village, every street would be blessed.

I shall not turn back!

It took Father Serra almost twenty years, from the time he was first summoned to come to the New World and serve in the missions, before he got to his first California Mission in San Diego, in what is today the State of California. Those twenty years prior to arriving at San Diego were at times a painful prelude, filled with joy and sorrows, readying him for his biggest challenge, setting up missions a day's walk apart up the coast of California. The missionary who worked furtively his last years on earth was tired and more dead than alive. When one of his companions begged him to stop, his legs so badly swollen and in pain that he could not celebrate Mass standing, Father Serra refused saying,

"Please do not speak of that, for I trust that if God will give me the strength to reach San Diego, as He has given me the strength to come this far, I shall not turn back. They can bury me wherever they wish and I shall gladly be left among the pagans, if it be the Will of God."

It had taken him almost three months to reach San Diego from Baja California. Half dead, most of the time, he never turned back!

December 26, 1770, Father Serra performed his first baptism in California. In addition to San Diego and San Carlos del Carmel, Father Serra went on to found San Antonio de Padua in July, 1771; San Gabriel in September, 1771; San Luis Obispo in September, 1772; San Francisco in October, 1776; San Juan Capistrano in January, 1777; and San Buenaventura in March 1782.

Our little missionary goes Home, at last!

August 28, 1784, with no more to give, his last ounce of blood shed for the Church he so passionately loved and brought to the natives of the Americas, Father Serra, died in the arms of his former student and dear friend Father Palóu.

Pressing his crucifix close to his heart, he turned to his friend and gave him his last will and testament:

"I promise, if the Lord in His infinite mercy grants me eternal happiness which I do not deserve because of my sins and faults, that I shall pray for all those (at the missions) and for the conversion of so many whom I have left unconverted."

Our missionary died as he lived, like Jesus before him, thinking and praying for those he was leaving behind. He taught the natives and by his example, as well as word, led them to become some of the strongest Catholics in the Western hemisphere.

Bibliography

Journey to Sainthood - Super Saints Book I
Galilea Segundo - *La Potenza e la Fragilità - Life of Mother Cabrini*
   Editrice Queriniana - Brescia, Italy 1993
Butler, Thurston & Atwater - *Lives of the Saints*
   Complete edition in 4 volumes - Christian Classics
   Westminster, Maryland 1980
Dirvin, Joseph L. - *Mrs. Seton*
   Basilica of Nat'l Shrine Elizabeth Seton - Emitsburg, MD 1993
Dirvin, Joseph L. - *The Soul of Elizabeth Seton*
   Ignatius Press, San Francisco 1990
Dolan, Sean - *Junípero Serra*
   Chelsea House Publishers - New York 1991
Dorcy Mary Jean Sr. OP - *Saint Dominic*
   Tan Publications, Rockford, IL 1982
History Cap du la Madeleine - Les Éditions Notre-Dame du Cap 1988
Bernardi, P.E. - *Leopoldo Mandic*
   Sanctuary of St. Leopoldo Mandic, Padua, Italy 1989
Giuditta Gardoni Bertolotti - *S. Angela Merici -*
   Editrice Àncora Milano - Milan, Italy 1971
Santi e Santuari # 41 - Milano Italy 1979

INDEX

Super Saints Trilogy

Journey to Sainthood
Founders, Confessors & Visionaries

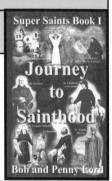
224 pages **Many Photos**

- Bl. Junipero Serra
- St. Frances (Mother) Cabrini
- St. Paschal Baylon
- St. Leopold Mandic
- St. Dominic

- St. Elizabeth Ann Seton
- St. Conrad
- St. Angela Merici
- Bl. Frederic

Holy Innocence
The Young and the Saintly

224 pages **Many Photos**

- St. Maria Goretti
- St. Aloysius Gonzaga
- St. Margaret of Castello
- St. Dominic Savio

- St. Gabriel Possenti
- St. Rose of Viterbo
- St. Stanislaus Kostka
- St. Philomena

Defenders of the Faith
Saints of the Counter-Reformation

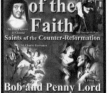
224 pages **Many Photos**

- St. Ignatius of Loyola
- St. Jane Frances de Chantal
- St. Charles Borromeo
- St. Teresa of Avila

- St. Pope Pius V
- St. Francis de Sales
- St. Vincent de Paul
- St. Philip Neri
- St. Robert Bellarmine

SUPER SAINTS TRILOGY
Three books at *Special Introductory* price
Call 1-800-633-2484 for details

Videos available based on this book

Bl. Junípero Serra
Bob & Penny Lord

V127 - Blessed Junípero Serra
Visit the **California Missions,** the legacy of **Blessed Junípero Serra**, apostle of California. See Mission **Santa Barbara, San Juan Capistrano** and Shrine at **Carmel Mission.**

Blessed Frederic
Bob & Penny Lord

V135 - Blessed Frédéric
Go to **Trois Rivieres** in Quebec, Canada, where **Bl. Frédéric** lived and is buried. See **Cap de la Madeleine,** where a huge Miracle took place. Venerate Our Lady at this Miraculous Shrine.

V150 - Saint Angela Merici
Foundress of Ursulines
Go to Northern Italy, Desezano, Brescia, Milan, Mantua and Rome. She had visions of Angels ascending and descending from Heaven.

St. Angela Merici
Bob & Penny Lord

St. Leopold Mandic
Bob & Penny Lord

V151 - Saint Leopold Mandic
Saint of Reconciliation Go to where he began in Herzegovina, to Venice and the Cathedral where he was ordained, to Padua. Visit his confessional, where he spent most of his life.

Mother Cabrini
Bob & Penny Lord

V155 - St. Frances (Mother) Cabrini
Follow her life from Sant' Angelo Lodigiano in northern Italy to her first community in Codogno, to the first motherhouse in Rome; then go to the United States.

St. Paschal Baylon
Bob & Penny Lord

V158 - Saint Paschal Baylon
St. Paschal Baylon is the Patron of Eucharistic Congresses and Confraternities of the Blessed Sacrament. Trace the life of this Defender of the Eucharist.

Bl. Elizabeth Ann Seton
Bob & Penny Lord

V161 - Elizabeth Ann Seton
Mother Seton is the first American-born Saint we have written about. Go to Emmitsburg, Maryland and the Shrine of this Saint and trace her life and works.

St. Dominic
Bob & Penny Lord

V188 - St. Dominic
Watchdog of God Trace the life of the founder of the Order of Preachers. Trace his life starting in Spain. He was given the Rosary by our lady and he fought the Albigensian Heresy.

Produced by Journeys of Faith®
To Order call 1-800-633-2484

Journeys of Faith®

To Order: 1-800-633-2484 FAX 916-853-0132 E-mail BPLord23@aol.com

Books

Bob and Penny Lord are authors of best sellers:

This Is My Body, This Is My Blood;
           Miracles of the Eucharist Book I $9.95 Paperback
This Is My Body, This Is My Blood;
           Miracles of the Eucharist Book II $13.95 Paperback
The Many Faces Of Mary, A Love Story $9.95 Paperback $13.95 Hardcover
We Came Back To Jesus $9.95 Paperback $13.95 Hardcover
Saints and Other Powerful Women in the Church $13.95 Paperback
Saints and Other Powerful Men in the Church $14.95 Paperback
Heavenly Army of Angels $13.95 Paperback
Scandal of the Cross and Its Triumph $13.95 Paperback
The Rosary - The Life of Jesus and Mary $13.95 Hardcover
Martyrs - They Died for Christ $13.95 Paperback
Visionaries, Mystics, and Stigmatists $13.95 Paperback
Visions of Heaven, Hell and Purgatory $13.95 Paperback
Treasures of the Church - That which makes us Catholic $9.95 Paperback
Tragedy of the Reformation $9.95 Paperback
Cults - Battle of the Angels $9.95 Paperback
Trilogy (3 Books - Treasure..., Tragedy... and Cults...) $25.00 Paperback
Journey to Sainthood - Founders, Confessors & Visionaries $10.95 Paperback
Holy Innocence - The Young and the Saintly $10.95 Paperback
Defenders of the Faith - Saints of the Counter-Reformation $10.95 Paperback
Super Saints Trilogy (3 Books - Journey ... Holy... Defenders...) $25.00

Please add $4.00 S&H for first book: $1.00 each add'l book

Videos and On-site Documentaries

Bob and Penny's Video Series based on their books:
13 part series on the Miracles of the Eucharist - 15 part series on The Many Faces of Mary - 23 part series on Martyrs - They Died for Christ - 10 part series on Visionaries, Mystics and Stigmatists - 50 part series on the Super Saints Trilogy
Many other on-site Documentaries based on Miracles of the Eucharist, Mother Mary's Apparitions, and the Heavenly Army of Angels. Request our list.

Our books and videos are available in Spanish also

Pilgrimages

Bob and Penny Lord's ministry take out Pilgrimages to the Shrines of Europe, and Mexico every year. Come and join them on one of these special Retreat Pilgrimages. Call for more information, and ask for the latest pilgrimage brochure.

Lecture Series

Bob and Penny travel to all parts of the world to spread the Good News. They speak on what they have written about in their books. If you would like to have them come to your area, call for information on a lecture series in your area.

Good Newsletter

We are publishers of the Good Newsletter, which is published four times a year. This newsletter will provide timely articles on our Faith, plus keep you informed with the activities of our community. Call 1-800-633-2484 for information.